VOCABBUSTERS
SAT Vol. 2

VOCABBUSTERS SAT Vol. 2

Dusti D. Howell, Ph.D.
Deanne K. Howell, M.S.

ISBN 9780967732879

Printed in the United States of America

Authors: Dusti D. Howell, Ph.D.
                    Deanne K. Howell, M.S.

Illustrators: James E. Rinehart II
                    Brad Williams

Cover Design: Another Design Guy, LLC

Book Layout: Robert Reiter

SolidA, Inc.
Address: 1717 Sherwood Way
                    Emporia, KS 66801

email: info@solida.net
Internet: http://www.solida.net

About the Authors

Dusti D. Howell, president of SolidA, has a Ph.D. in Educational Communications and Technology and a Ph.D. minor in Educational Psychology from the University of Wisconsin-Madison. Much of his research was done at Emporia State University as an Associate Professor in the Instructional Design and Technology Department. His expertise also includes innovations and research in high-tech study skills and digital learning strategies. Dusti has taught every grade level from first grade to graduate school.

Deanne K. Howell has earned a Masters Degree in Curriculum and Instruction from the University of Wisconsin-Madison. She is also an educator with experience teaching elementary through graduate classes.

Dusti and Deanne have published numerous books and articles, and have developed a number of workshops and multimedia programs.

SolidA, Inc. is dedicated to improving student learning with technology and scientific research. Our passion is to help learners succeed. Our goal is to help students get Solid A's.

Special Acknowledgments

We would like to express our sincere gratitude to:

Bob Reiter for his tireless work formatting the layout of this book.

Jim Rinehart and Brad Williams who brought humor and life to our words through their cartoon illustrations.

John C. Lehman, Communications Professor at Emporia State University, for generously donating his time and talent to the audio recordings.

Brenda Gray, for her work with the voice narrations.

Merriam-Webster, Incorporated for permission to use their written pronunciations throughout this book.

Julie Rosenquist and Ginger Lewman for their input and advise on this project.

We are also thankful for Rachel Haskins and Cecelia White's assistance.

Table of Contents

Fun while learning vocabulary?

Vocabbusters introduces new words using a fun, multisensory approach.
* Each word is illustrated with a cartoon.
* Memory devices (mnemonics) are used to help you further remember and learn each word.
* Understand how each word is used in context with example sentences taken from major books and publications.
* Avoid mispronunciations by listening to the audio recordings.
* Enjoy watching select words come to life with clever animations that are sure to make you smile.
* Crossword puzzles, Matching Activies, and Multiple Choice Quizzes are included for review.
* Make up your own vocabulary cards by using the VOCABBUSTERS template at the back of this book.
* Learn how to search GoogleBooks to find your own words used in context.

For more free resources visit, http://www.solida.net

Introducing the VOCABBUSTERS Methodology

Learning vocabulary does not have to be difficult or dull. VOCABBUSTERS is based on over two decades of research on vocabulary acquisition, retention and usage. The strategies used in this book have been statistically proven to be superior learning devices for building vocabulary. VOCABBUSTERS combines two of the best methods to assist you in learning new words—the Keyword and Semantic-Context methods. The presentation of this information, centered on a cartoon, creates a memorable visual mnemonic. Audio recordings enable students to hear the words in order to pronounce the words correctly. Kinesthetic activities help to make learning easier and more fun.

Why is having a good vocabulary important?

Vocabulary acquisition is the single best indicator of intelligence and IQ according to Robert Sternberg, an Educational Psychologist at Yale University. Extensive portions of college entrance exams, including the S.A.T. and G.R.E., use vocabulary testing as a measure to predict academic performance. More importantly, simply reading does not guarantee a good vocabulary (Sternberg, 1986), which means that strategies for acquiring vocabulary need to be taught. Unfortunately, most schools do not devote any time for teaching effective techniques for learning vocabulary. When learning new vocabulary words, most students are left to rely on rote memorization, unaware that more efficient strategies are available. Therefore their vocabulary suffers, and in the end, many students remain ill prepared for college, and subsequently become more limited with their career choices.

VOCABBUSTERS is Simply the Best!

There are two simple reasons why VOCABBUSTERS is the best method for learning new vocabulary words. First, VOCABBUSTERS is two scientific methodologies built into one. By combining two of the most empirically validated methods for learning vocabulary into one simple interface, we have significantly increased the learner's chances for success. Second, we have added visual, auditory and kinesthetic supports to allow learners multiple "brain based" pathways for learning new words. That means you can study with just your strongest sensory style, or you can utilize all three sensory modalities. It all depends on what works best for you. For example, an auditory learner can just listen to the online audio files, or s/he can study the visual cartoons and easily utilize the kinesthetic techniques to quickly find dozens of example sentences online and then write a favorite one down at the bottom of each page. Again, our purpose is to easily provide the tools to allow you to study in the way that best suits your style of learning, thereby increasing your chances for success. Let's take a look at the two reasons why VOCABBUSTERS is the best in greater detail.

1) Combing the Best Methods

Numerous research articles have been written to prove the veracity of one method over another. It is interesting to note that in these "Battles of the Methods" two methods have been studied in great detail—the Keyword and Semantic-Context methods. In much of the research, the keyword method was shown to be very strong and empirically the best method for learning new vocabulary. However, over time, studies have shown semantic-context to be an excellent method, and in some cases as good as the keyword approach. A more detailed analysis of the strengths and weaknesses of each method led to an interesting discovery. The major strengths of each method complemented and added value to the other method. By juxtapositioning (combining) these two methods, the user will be able to easily remember definitions (keyword strength) and apply them in daily communications (semantic-context strength). For years these methods have been battling it out to see which one is the best. It is almost like comparing peanut butter and jelly. However, by combining the two methods into one new method, VOCABBUSTERS gives students a stronger base of research on which to rely.

The Keyword Method

The first step in using this method is to find a keyword for the word you are trying to learn. For example, let's say you're trying to learn the word *olfactory*. A good keyword for the word *olfactory* is *oil factory* because it follows three rules.

1. The word sounds acoustically similar to the target word.
2. The word is a concrete noun, which makes it easier to draw or visualize.
3. The word is common or familiar to the learner.

The second step is to link the keyword to the target definition. More simply, we need to link the word *oil factory* to "sense of smell." Visualize watching smoke spewing from an oil factory and smelling really bad. Draw a simple picture that depicts this situation and add the caption "That *oil factory* is bothering my *olfactory* sense." This visual mnemonic will assist the learner in remembering the meaning of the new word.

The final step is to practice recalling the target word. When you think of *olfactory*, first think of the keyword (*oil factory*), then remember what was happening in the picture (smoke is spewing out and smells bad), and finally that *olfactory* means *sense of smell.*

When tested against other methods, the keyword strategy repeatedly proved to be a superior technique for acquiring vocabulary for subjects of nearly all ages, and with periodic review, one of the best methods for long-term retention. The strength of this mnemonic strategy is in aiding the learner in remembering the definition of vocabulary words. Mnemonic strategies work! In fact, Purdue University researchers' Mastropieri and Scruggs (1991), "never found a 'type of learner' who could not benefit from mnemonic instruction." Additionally, the subjects in these studies not only liked the use of the strategy but expressed greater enjoyment in learning.

Semantic-Context Method

To learn a word using this method, context clues are placed in the sentence to help the learner define the word. For example, try to figure out what olfactory means from the following sentence. "His *olfactory* sense told him that someone had been smoking in the room." Clues within the sentence help the user define the meaning as "the sense of smell."

The semantic-context method has been identified as one of the best learning devices and has tested as one of the best strategies for delayed recall. Strictly speaking, in this book, only the first example sentence uses the semantic-context method. We created these sentences so that the target words were used within a meaningful context. We added two additional sentences from print sources that demonstrated real life examples. Although some of these sentences could also be considered semantic-context, only the first example sentence was strictly created for that purpose. These sentences as a whole should aid learners in actively integrating these words into their working vocabulary, using them on a daily basis.

2) Study with Style

What's your cognitive style? Do you learn best when you see an illustration depicting the meaning of a new word (visual), when you hear the new word being used (auditory), or when you find an example of the word used in real life and write it down (kinesthetic)? By providing visual cartoons, audio narrations and kinesthetic activities, we allow users to study with their primary learning styles. Keyword mnemonics create excellent visual links connecting keywords to the definitions of the targeted vocabulary word. This visual approach is best for recalling word definitions. We created the audio from the caption sentences of the cartoons and from each semantic-context sentence (first example sentence for each word). Auditory learners should find these extremely helpful in learning these words. Finally, kinesthetic learners can follow the directions on page fourteen to quickly find dozens of example sentences online and then write a favorite one down at the bottom of each page.

Many will certainly find it useful to integrate all three of these approaches into the learning process for each word. By listening to the recordings while reading over the sentences and studying the cartoon, and then searching through lists of example sentences and selecting one to write down, users will be storing this information in multiple locations of their brain. Proponents of dual coding theory claim that multimedia enhanced lessons can help strengthen the learning process by processing the same information in multiple areas of the brain, including the visual and auditory cortexes. Even more than dual coding, perhaps those that use all three approaches are using triple coding. Either way, every one of these supports is given with the goal of giving learners multiple methods to succeed.

VOCABBUSTERS Caters to all Types of Learners.

Here's how VOCABBUSTERS engages the three primary senses in learning new words.

> ### What's Your Cognitive Style?
> Find out free at www.solida.net

Visual Learners learn best when they see a visual image or picture. The cartoon illustrations for each word create a humorous and memorable way for learning new words. When trying to recall the meaning of a word, visual learners should try to remember the keyword and the related cartoon that illustrates the word. Recalling the activity in the cartoon helps visual learners remember the meaning of the target word. Additionally, visual learners might find it beneficial to color the pictures in the book.

Auditory Learners- Audio files increase learning and eliminate the guess work from determining pronunciations. Students no longer need to worry about whether they are mispronouncing words. According to middle school teacher Ginger Lewman, "I've had kids work on words by themselves and come back to me mispronouncing them. For instance, the word facade (pronounced f&-'säd) becomes f&-'kAd. Now that could be VERY embarrassing on down the road and discourage them from trying to learn new words on their own." With the audio recordings, auditory learners can easily learn new words independently and pronounce them correctly. Students with auditory preferences can review words by listening to them at any time.

Watch and listen to additional SAT words come to life in funny animated cartoons at http://www.solida.net.

Kinesthetic Learners- Interact with the words by creating additional example sentences for each word. A great way to do this is to use *Google Books*. Google Books is a completely free online search engine that enables users to search inside books for pages that include a particular word. Here's how to use this valuable tool:

1. Go to Google's Books website at http://books.google.com.
2. If you are searching for the word **baleful**, type **baleful** in the Google Search Books window and press "Search Books."
3. Pick your favorite sentence from this list and write it in the "write your own" section provided at the bottom of the page.

Use the VOCABBUSTERS template at the back of this book to make your own "VOCABBUSTERS" or visit http://www.solida.net to print a PDF file.

For additional kinesthetic activities solve the crossword puzzles and take the matching and multiple choice quizzes at the end of the chapters. Also try to Listen to the recordings while moving about.

Pronunciation Guide

Many words have more than one correct pronunciation. In this book we have included one or two of the most common pronunciations for each word.

(http://www.m-w.com/cgi-bin/dictionary#)

\&\ as **a** and **u** in abut	\ᵃ\ as **e** in kitten	\&r\ as **ur/er** in further
\a\ as **a** in ash	\A\ as **a** in ace	\ä\ as **o** in mop
\au\ as **ou** in out	\ch\ as **ch** in chin	\e\ as **e** in bet
\E\ as **ea** in easy	\g\ as **g** in go	\i\ as **i** in hit
\I\ as **i** in ice	\j\ as **j** in job	\[ng]\ as **ng** in sing
\O\ as **o** in go	\o\ as **aw** in law	\oi\ as **oy** in boy
\th\ as **th** in thin	\[th]\ as **th** in the	\ü\ as **oo** in loot
\u\ as **oo** in foot	\y\ as **y** in yet	\zh\ as **si** in vision

By permission of the publisher. From Merriam-Webster's Online Dictionary at http://www.merriam-webster.com by Merriam-Webster, Incorporated.

How to Review

Try to recall as much information about each word before looking at the page. You may wish to cover up the page, with only the target vocabulary word visible. Try to recall each part before uncovering it. To review the word *olfactory*:

1. Recall the keyword [oil factory]
2. Visualize the cartoon picture of the sun inhaling the fumes from the smelly oil factory.
3. Connect the picture to the meaning of the target word [referring to the sense of smell]
4. Think about how the word was used in a sentence or try to make up a sentence of your own.

VOCABBUSTERS Sample Overview

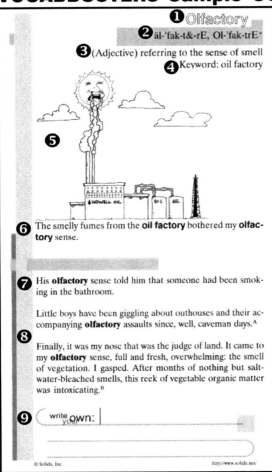

❶ Olfactory

❷ äl-'fak-t&-rE, Ol-'fak-trE*

❸ (Adjective) referring to the sense of smell

❹ Keyword: oil factory

❺

❻ The smelly fumes from the **oil factory** bothered my **olfactory** sense.

❼ His **olfactory** sense told him that someone had been smoking in the bathroom.

❽ Little boys have been giggling about outhouses and their accompanying **olfactory** assaults since, well, caveman days.[A]

Finally, it was my nose that was the judge of land. It came to my **olfactory** sense, full and fresh, overwhelming: the smell of vegetation. I gasped. After months of nothing but saltwater-bleached smells, this reek of vegetable organic matter was intoxicating.[B]

❾ write your own: |

© Solida, Inc.   http://www.solida.net/

1. Target word
2. Pronunciations are from the experts at Merriam-Webster. Many words have more than one pronunciation.
3. Part of speech and definition.
4. The keyword consists of a word or short phrase that sounds similar to the target word.
5. Cartoon illustration links the target word to the keyword and definition.
6. The cartoon caption ties the target word to the keyword and definition.
7. The target word used within a meaningful sentence (Semantic Context).
8. Two example sentences taken from leading books or publications.
9. Create your own sentence using the target word. Use the directions on page xii to find great example sentences.

Section One

Abeyance

&-'bA-&nts   or   &-'bA-&ns

(Noun) a temporary suspension (interruption)
of function or activity
Keyword: advance

The runners were held in **abeyance** and were not allowed to **advance** due to the construction of the bridge.

The dance was held in **abeyance**--temporarily postponed until a band could be found.

Summer is finally a-coming in, just in time for the annual open-air symphony concerts. In Melbourne, this tradition has been in **abeyance** for two years while the Sidney Myer Music Bowl has been refurbished [restored or fixed up]....[1]

She has created a few areas in which she lets go of that practical, conservative side, in particular a lifelong love of sports cars (currently in **abeyance** with a city-owned car and family minivan).[2]

write your own:

Abhor

&b-'hor or ab-'hor

(Verb) to hate or to detest strongly
Keyword: a bore

The students **abhorred** class because their teacher was such **a bore**.

Frank **abhors** swimming class because he is afraid of the water.

The guilty **abhor** silence. It makes them uncomfortable.[3]

The question is whether, in pursuing them, he demonstrates the strong leadership that Americans admire or overreaches in a way that voters will **abhor**.[4]

write your own: |

Abrogate

'a-br&-"gAt

(Verb) to end; to abolish formally,
or to officially get rid of
Keyword: afro date

The afro date law requiring all students to have an **afro** hair style in order to **date** was **abrogated** after several new bald students came to the school.

In an attempt to **abrogate** all speeding, the local police force was heavily patrolling all the streets in our town.

It is not fair to hold every parent responsible for a child's misfortunes, but neither can a parent **abrogate** his or her protective role....[5]

There really was a Sheriff of Nottingham, though: his name, Philip Mark, even appears in the Magna Carta, a landmark document drawn up by rebellious lords seeking to **abrogate** the absolute power of tyrants [all powerful rulers] like Philip's employer, King John.[6]

write your own: |

Abstract

ab-'strakt or 'ab-"strakt

(Noun) summary including the most important points/
Keyword: subtract

Note: Abstract can also mean "considered apart from a concrete existence/difficult to understand"

To create an **abstract**, **subtract** most of the words.

The scientific journal began each article with a brief **abstract** that summarized the article in a few sentences.

According to the **abstract**, the authors wanted to test the commonly held notion that noses and ears get bigger as people grow older, so they measured these appendages among 100 young people and compared them with those of 100 old people.[7]

Despite shortness—one paragraph of 24 lines—the **abstract** contained an enormous amount of new science:....[8]

write your own: |

Adulation

a-j&-'lA-sh&n or "a-dy&-'lA-sh&n

(Noun) excessive flattery or praise, often undeserved

Keyword: add a nation

When the United Nations **adds a nation** to its coalition, the members applaud with **adulation**.

Juan adored the **adulation** he received for being the best guitar player in his group.

Ted Turner, billionaire media mogul and legendary yachtsman, came to town for a regatta [sports meeting] last weekend and received predictable **adulation** from the city's sailing community.[9]

Personal humility demonstrates a compelling modesty, shunning [avoiding] public **adulation**: never boastful.[10]

write your own:

Alacrity

&-'la-kr&-tE

(Noun) cheerful readiness or willingness; responding promptly.

Keyword: a lack of tea

When there was **a lack of tea**, the guests accepted the offer of coffee with great **alacrity**.

After winning the lottery, Darin accepted the significant sum of cash with great **alacrity**.

The film, which focused on the work of the Red Cross, captured [Princess] Diana's imagination and she agreed with **alacrity** to help raise funds in the campaign to rid the world of landmines.[11]

Dog owners have taken to the target stick with **alacrity**. One can use a target stick to teach a rambunctious, out-of-control dog to walk nicely in heel position.[12]

write your own: _____

Alienate

'A-lE-&-"nAt or 'Al-y&-"nAt

(Verb) to separate in an unfriendly or hostile manner
Keyword: alien

The **aliens'** strange and bizarre mannerisms **alienated** them from the human population.

Her terrible table manners in the cafeteria helped further **alienate** her from her classmates.

In our lives there are genuine religious, ethnic and political differences that separate and even **alienate** us from others.[13]

They threatened to **alienate** their most beloved figure, George Brett, now the team's vice president of baseball operations, by firing his longtime friend, bench coach Jamie Quirk.[14]

write your own: |

Ambivalence

am-'bi-v&l&nts or am-'bi-v&-l&ns

(Noun) two opposing feelings held simultaneously
(at the same time)/ uncertainty
Keyword: ambulance

The **ambulance** driver felt a strange **ambivalence** as he struggled to decide whether to take the robber to the hospital or to the police station.

The mother felt a strange sense of **ambivalence** when it was time to send her child off to college. She was happy to see her receive a good education, but she also felt sad to see her leave.

Frank feels a deep **ambivalence** about leaving ... He is both sad to go but relieved to get on with defending himself.[15]

It's about her own **ambivalence** doing something that makes her feel good and at the same time truly frightens her.[16]

write your own:

Amorphous

&-'mor-f&s

(Adjective) having no distinct or
definite form or shape
Keyword: a porpoise

The **amorphous** clouds suddenly took shape and re-sembled **a porpoise**.

Shelly tried several times to clean the **amorphous** ink blot stain on her couch.

The High Court effectively found that the worldwide web is not quite so borderless and **amorphous** as some of its adherents have claimed.[17]

The electron doesn't fly around the nucleus like a planet around its sun, but instead takes on the more **amorphous** aspect of a cloud.[18]

write your own: |

©Solid A, Inc.   http://SolidA.net

Anomaly

&-'nä-m&-lE

(Noun) someone or something that is uncommon or irregular

Keyword: anemone

The discovery of the sea **anemones** was an **anomaly** in the fresh water lake.

Scientists had performed the experiment repeatedly with the same results, but this time something was different. The results were an **anomaly**.

The vampire bats are pretty darn cool, the exotic birds are beautiful, and the guy in the scuba gear cleaning the tank was an interesting **anomaly**, looking klutzy among more graceful (albeit confined) creatures.[19]

His pediatrician picked up an **anomaly** in his heart during a routine checkup. The cardiologist confirmed that [he] had several holes in his heart.[20]

write your own:

Apathy

'a-p&-thE

(Noun) lack of feeling or interest
Keyword: a path

After traveling thousands of miles on **a path**, the pioneers started developing a feeling of **apathy** towards finishing their journey.

The school decided to cancel the chess club pep rally due to student **apathy** towards the activity.

Once an energetic, optimistic manager, Jim began complaining of fatigue, and his general **apathy** led to lost accounts and missed publication deadlines.[21]

The fact that his part of town, or any other, does not have libraries, parks, good roads or even good security is ... because of big—and I mean big—voter **apathy**.[22]

write your own:

Apocryphal

&-'pä-kr&-f&l

(Adjective) false; not genuine
Keyword: a pocket full

The young boy had **a pocket full** of **apocryphal** diamonds which he sold to his classmates, even though they were fake.

Many urban legends are spread via email. These **apocryphal** hoaxes can quickly be debunked at an urban legend website.

Preparing us against snakebite, Japper had brought a battery-powered cattle prod. If applied quickly, he said, the electrical shock would mitigate [minimize] the effect of a bite. Fortunately we never had to test this **apocryphal** snakebite remedy.[23]

When the Lutheran minister came to his house in St. Louis to recruit my grandmother, he beat him up. Maybe it's an **apocryphal** family legend....[24]

write your own:

Arduous

'är-j&-w&s or 'är-dyu-w&s

(Adjective) difficult to do; requiring great effort/ steep
Keyword: card to us

The 300 page **card to us** was an **arduous** undertaking. It looked more like a book than a get well card.

Though the hike up the mountain was long and **arduous**, it was well worth it to see the view from the top.

This situation is changing, however, as researchers begin systematically to probe Antarctica's ice, rock and sediments for clues. Their work is always **arduous**, often heroic and sometimes dangerous.[25]

Construction companies aim to create long-term bonds with clients that will reap repeat jobs and, perhaps, eliminate the **arduous** bidding process.[26]

write your own:

Assiduous

&-'sij-w&s or &-'si-j&-w&s

(Adjective) persistent; diligent; constant attention
Keyword: acid

To determine the effects of acid on limestone, the scientist had the **assiduous** task of adding **acid** to the limestone every half hour for two weeks.

The college students were **assiduous** in their year long fight for better food in the cafeteria.

[Thomas] Jefferson described [Meriwether Lewis] as "an **assiduous** and attentive farmer, observing with minute attention all plants and insects he met with."[27]

Grimm is clearly an **assiduous** scholar of Elizabethan literary language, and he mimics it with impressive determination.[28]

write your own: |

Attenuation

&-"ten-y&-'wA-sh&n

(Noun) the act of making thinner, smaller or weaker

Keyword: a tent station

Due to the **attenuated** budget for the radio station, the D.J. saved money by working in **a tent station** in his backyard.

The hikers were shocked at the **attenuation** of their food supply after only three days of camping.

During that time, Pasteur enhanced the concept of **attenuation**, which is the use of a weakened form of a virus to provide immunity. Pasteur found that a weakened form of chicken cholera (an **attenuated** form) was highly effective in preventing the disease. **Attenuated** vaccines are widely used today.[29]

Indeed, it is not unknown for the shade temperature in the city to be a little lower than in the surrounding countryside ... because of the slight **attenuation** of the city sunlight by the dust and smoke endemic [prevalent in] in the urban atmosphere.[30]

write your own:

Attribution

"a-tr&-'byü-sh&n

(Noun) the act of giving due credit to a
particular person or group
Keyword: hat pollution

Attribution for the poisoned water was placed on the hat
factory that dumped their out dated hats in the river. This
was a case of "**hat pollution.**"

The anonymous author of the famous poem was finally identified and given due **attribution** for her work.

Correction: Because of an editing error, the **attribution** of
the source of information in a graphic ... in last week's Health-
Science section was incorrect.[31]

When things go well, you look through the window; in other
words, you look at everyone out there all they did to con-
tribute, and you give them credit, **attribution**, recognition,
acknowledgment, and appreciation.[32]

write own:

Audacious

o-'dA-sh&s

(Adjective) bold or adventurous
Keyword: all day shifts

The **audacious** mountain rescue job required workers to be able to handle **all day shifts**, 24 hours straight, under the worst of conditions.

Though Bill's **audacious** idea was initially dismissed as being too bold and dangerous, his friends started to come around later.

The proposal was **audacious** — the New Orleans Saints offering to trade all of their 1999 draft picks, plus future considerations, for the chance to select Heisman Trophy-winning running back Ricky Williams of Texas.[33]

Days of **audacious** daylight robberies, thwarted by Marines, have left two blocks of the district a gutted [looted] ruin. [34]

write your own:

Aver

&-'v&r

(Verb) to verify or confirm the truth
Keyword: love her

WOW! YOU REALLY DO LOVE ME!

He was finally able to **aver** his **love** to **her**, when he proposed marriage.

After being accused of breaking the window, the child **averred**
and apologized for throwing the ball.

The black huckleberry ... is the most popular, but Fernald
and Kinsey **aver** that the dangleberry ... is just as good and
will make one of the most luscious of deserts, being remarkably juicy and with a rich spicy flavor.[35]

Akagi's log (journal) **avers** that she saw the attackers fifty
kilometers out.[36]

write your own:

'bAn

(Noun) the cause of injury or mischief

Keyword: brain

The cigarette smoke was a **bane** to his **brain**, and gave him the worst headache.

Fans who don't want to pay for CDs or MP3s anymore are the current **bane** of the music industry.

The disruption of your body's sleep cycle after along transcontinental flight-better known as jet lag-is the **bane** of every business traveler.[37]

Economically, we are the **bane**, not the hope of the world. Since the planet is finite [limited], as we expand our economy we make it less likely that less developed nations can expand theirs.[38]

write your own:

Bellicose

'be-li-"kOs

(Adjective) warlike or aggressive
Keyword: bells in clothes

The eerie sound of the **bells in clothes** could be heard as the **bellicose** invaders marched closer.

Some of the child's actions and statements were so **bellicose** that his parents were forced to have the child see a counselor before he attacked someone.

One afternoon he was riding home on a suburban Tokyo train when a huge, **bellicose**, and very drunk laborer got on. The man began terrorizing the passengers: screaming curses....[39]

So the writer has to take the most used, most familiar objects; nouns, pronouns, verbs, adverbs, ...and make people get into a romantic mood; and another way, into a **bellicose** mood.[40]

write your own: |_____

Section 1 Crossword Puzzle

Across

5. to hate; to detest strongly

8. a temporary interruption of function or activity

9. someone or something that is uncommon or irregular

10. the cause of injury or mischief

12. persistent; diligent; constant attention

14. the act of giving due credit to a particular person or group

15. false; not genuine

17. the act of making thinner, smaller, or weaker

Down

1. cheerful readiness or willingness; responding promptly

2. two opposing feelings held at the same time/ uncertainty

3. warlike or aggressive

4. to separate in an unfriendly hostile manner

5. bold or adventurous

6. excessive flattery or praise, often undeserved

7. difficult to do; requiring great effort/ steep

8. summary including the most important point

11. to verify or confirm the truth

12. having no distinct or definite form

13. to end; to abolish formally or to officially get rid of

16. lack of feeling or interest

Section 1 Multiple Choice Review

Select the word that best fits each sentence.

1. Musical sensation Cat Stevens _____ himself from many of his fans when he suddenly stopped singing his popular songs.
   a. averred   b. alienated   c. attenuated   d. abrogated

2. The _____ lawyer worked tirelessly for two months in order to prepare his defense.
   a. arduous   b. apocryphal   c. audacious   d. assiduous

3. The news aired a short _____ of the President's speech.
   a. abstract   b. attribution   c. anomaly   d. apathy

4. Because he had never studied art, Bart could not understand why the colorful, _____ blobs of clay were on display in a museum.
   a. averred   b. arduous   c. bane   d. amorphous

5. Katie began to _____ her step-mother when she repeatedly made her do all the housework.
   a. adulate   b. abrogate   c. abhor   d. alienate

6. The tradition of eating turkey on Thanksgiving in my family was _____ after my parents became vegetarians.
   a. abrogated   b. averred   c. apocryphal   d. alienated

7. Though they rarely receive _____, teachers remain an integral part of a child's life.
   a. attenuation   b. abeyance   c. alacrity   d. adulation

8. Dena drove to the airport with great _____ because she was so excited to see her friend after being apart for three years.
   a. apathy   b. alacrity   c. attenuation   d. audacity

9. After incorrectly being accused of cheating, the student _____ that the answers were his own by showing his worksheet.
   a. averred   b. abrogated   c. adulated   d. abhorred

10. In the past, _____ for the great work of art had been bestowed on the wrong person. Someone different had actually created it.
    a. attenuation   b. abeyance   c. attribution   d. abstraction

11. Attempting to start a water balloon fight, Jerry made some _____ comments that would entice his hopeful opponents to participate.
   a. bellicose   b. arduous   c. ambivalent   d. assiduous

12. While waiting to find out if she got the part in the play, Amy tried to keep her nervousness in _____.
   a. abeyance   b. attribution   c. ambivalence   d. aversion

13. Because the new employee wore such crazy clothes, he was considered a(n) _____ in the office.
   a. bane   b. anomaly   c. attribution   d. amorphous

14. Though many of the stories passed down in my family have always been held to be true, if any research is done on them they will probably be found to be _____.
   a. abstracted   b. audacious   c. apocryphal   d. assiduous

15. Though the trip was expected to be a(n) _____ adventure, it ended up being easy.
   a. bellicose   b. bemused   c. arduous   d. bane

16. The prisoners planned a(n) _____ escape that cut through the adjoining guard station.
   a. assiduous   b. abhorrent   c. bellicose   d. audacious

17. Experiencing frequent migraines is the _____ of my existence.
   a. bane   b. anomaly   c. alienation   d. aversion

18. Because Linda felt _____ towards gardening, weeds invaded her yard.
   a. adulation   b. bellicose   c. attribution   d. apathy

19. The customer was in such a state of _____ that he was unable to decide between coffee and tea.
   a. bellicose   b. abeyance   c. alacrity   d. ambivalence

20. By dropping two classes, the student felt less stressed due to her _____ class load.
   a. attenuated   b. abrogated   c. anomalous   d. apocryphal

Section 1 Matching Review

Directions: Match each word with its correct meaning.

1. _____ Abeyance
2. _____ Abhor
3. _____ Abrogate
4. _____ Abstract
5. _____ Adulation
6. _____ Alacrity
7. _____ Alienate
8. _____ Ambivalence
9. _____ Amorphous
10. _____ Anomaly
11. _____ Apathy
12. _____ Apocryphal
13. _____ Arduous
14. _____ Assiduous
15. _____ Attenuation
16. _____ Attribution
17. _____ Audacious
18. _____ Aver
19. _____ Bane
20. _____ Bellicose

A. two opposing feelings held simultaneously; uncertainty
B. warlike or aggressive
C. to end; to abolish formally or to officially get rid of
D. difficult to do; requiring great effort/ steep
E. a temporary suspension of function or activity
F. the act of making thinner, smaller, or weaker
G. the act of giving due credit to a particular person or group
H. having no distinct or definite form
I. bold or adventurous
J. summary including the most important points/ considered apart from a concrete existence
K. cheerful readiness or willingness; responding promptly
L. someone or something that is uncommon or irregular
M. excessive flattery or praise, often undeserved
N. lack of feeling or interest
O. persistent; diligent; constant attention
P. false; not genuine
Q. to verify or confirm the truth
R. to hate; to detest strongly
S. the cause of injury or mischief
T. to separate in an unfriendly or hostile manner

Section Two

Bemuse

bi-'myüz

(Verb) to confuse or stupefy/ absorb in thought
Keyword: be a moose

The park ranger was **bemused** to learn that he would have to **be a moose** to follow the migratory patterns of the herd.

I was **bemused** by Lisa's sudden rage at me. I thought we were friends.

You can park overnight for free at a gas station by putting a note under your wiper that says you broke down and have gone for help. Usually, people break down and walk to a gas station, so this reversal of logic will baffle and **bemuse** the attendants. [42]

Allende knows that the view she offers is hazy, but she wants it that way. Her aim in this nonfiction memoir of the spirits is not to clarify but to obscure, to emphasize and, as she says, to invent her native country so as to **bemuse** us. [41]

write your own: |

Bequeath

bi-'kwEth or bi-'kwE[th]

(Verb) to arrange to leave possessions, property, or money to others after death

Keyword: big wreath

He **bequeathed** his **big wreath** to his grandchild after he died.

In his will, Grandpa **bequeathed** his beloved coin collection to his grandsons.

On September 11, he wrote his last will and testament: "I **bequeath** all my estate, real and personal, to my mother...."[43]

As a boy [he] used to wander in the lush greenery of his father's 3,000 date palm trees. He could never have imagined then that wars would someday destroy the huge, thriving date industry here, leaving him a single tree to **bequeath** to his grandson.[44]

write your own: |

Breach

(Noun) the act of breaking or state
of being broken/ a gap
Keyword: beach

As a result of the earthquake a large **breach** appeared on
the **beach**.

Police cars were outside the bank within minutes after being
notified that there was a security **breach** within.

People on the receiving end are franker about stating the size
they expect those tips to be and using embarrassment to pressure tippers into giving more. A particularly insidious [tricky]
technique in vogue [current trend] now is to refrain from offering change and then loudly asking whether the customer "wants"
it, as if taking it would be a **breach** of manners.[45]

"The most surprising thing in my mind was that almost 30% of
the companies surveyed did have a **breach** of security last
year...."[46]

write your own:

46 ©Solid A, Inc.   http://SolidA.net

Burnish

'b&r-nish

(Verb) to polish especially by rubbing
Keyword: burned dish

After the candles **burned** the **dish**, mother **burnished** it with a polishing cloth until it shined like new.

Matt enjoyed helping his father clean and **burnish** his valuable coins.

Unlike some colored-pencil artists, [she] does not **burnish** layers of color with white, because she finds that it can alter the colors too much.[47]

[He] could try to buy back the Rolls name from BMW before 2003. BMW might be willing—it doesn't need another luxury nameplate to **burnish** its already polished image.[48]

write your own: _____

Cacophony

ka-'kä-f&-nE or ka-'ko-f&-nE

(Noun) a harsh assortment of
loud and unpleasant sounds
Keyword: cough funny

"You **cough funny**!" exclaimed Bob as his friend coughed and disturbed the library with a loud **cacophony** of harsh sounds.

The elementary band sounded more like a **cacophony** of random sounds, rather than music.

The arena's in-house restaurant and bar filled with a **cacophony** of noise when, on the television screens overhead, unheralded [unpredicted] Los Angeles Kings forward Mikko Eloranta scored on Dan Cloutier of Vancouver...[49]

Amid the dusty bedlam [chaos] of Kathmandu's neighborhood, [was] a **cacophony** of motorcycle engines, truck horns, rooster calls, police whistles, fruit hawkers, and chanting sidewalk monks fill the kerosene-laced air....[50]

write your own:

          http://SolidA.net

Candor

'kan-d&r or 'kan-"dor

(Noun) truthfulness or sincerity
Keyword: canned dirt

The company confessed with **candor** that the idea to market **canned dirt** was bad.

The parent was able to talk about his child's misbehavior with more **candor** than the school administration would have expected.

When Duke University surgeons last month transplanted an incompatible set of organs into [the] teenager ... who would later die, the doctors and hospital publicly confessed the mix-up and apologized. Such **candor** is part of a growing trend among hospitals to own up to the truth when patients are harmed....[51]

It is clear that after Ford was named vice president, a change came over his wife. Slowly, she [Betty Ford] was beginning to revert back to the woman she had been before she married Gerald Ford-a self-assured woman of **candor** who enjoyed the spotlight.[52]

write your own: |

Capricious

k&-'pri-sh&s or k&-'prE-sh&s

(Adjective) unpredictable, whimsical, or impulsive

Keyword: cup of fishes

Because the **capricious** children could not decide on a fish to buy, the pet store owner gave them a **cup of fishes** to take home.

The mother was unable to please her **capricious** daughter, who always wanted a different toy.

It is generally agreed that the weather of spring is not to be relied upon. Or, to put it another way, it is to be relied upon— to be utterly **capricious**, mean and nasty one moment, smiles and sweetness the next, like little girls.[53]

It is possible for the lady to be hostile, fiercely independent, passive, feminine, aggressive and warm. Of course at any particular moment would not be **capricious**— it would depend on who she is with, when, how, and much more.[54]

write your own: |

Castigate

'kas-t&-"gAt

(Verb) to punish or criticize harshly
Keyword: cast on a gate

The doctor **castigated** the patient for fooling around and ultimately breaking his **cast on a gate**.

After the accident, the owner of the amusement park was **castigated** for not meeting the safety regulations.

Unlucky persons are likely to **castigate** themselves with thoughts of "This need not have happened" or "I brought this on myself."[55]

It is easy to point at the public offender and **castigate** him in shame and judgment.[56]

write your own: _____

Coalesce

"kO-&-'les

(Verb) to unite, merge, or bring together into one
Keyword: coal less (less coal)

With **less coal** in the community, the union leaders and management agreed to **coalesce** to solve the problem.

The football team finally **coalesced** and began playing like a unified unit.

According Hoyle's theory, an exploding star would generate enough heat to create all the new elements and spray them into the cosmos where they would form gaseous clouds and could eventually **coalesce** into new solar systems.[57]

The Sibelius boasted the best playing I've ever heard from the National Symphony Orchestra. This is a wonderful piece, almost minimalist [moderate] in the way it is constructed from modules [elements] of sound that **coalesce** into a statement of grandeur [magnificence].[58]

write your own:

©Solid A, Inc.   http://SolidA.net

Cognizant

'käg-n&-z&nt

(Adjective) having knowledge of something; informed
Keyword: cog is bent

The wheel maker is **cognizant** of the fact that the **cog is bent** and is in need of repair.

The children were not **cognizant** that a big surprise was planned for them and waiting just around the corner.

Rather than just we veterans, everyone is more **cognizant** of what Memorial Day means this year....[59]

Scott's wife and children know better than to interrupt the Nets' coach when he's scouting potential opponents for next week's conference finals.—"Everybody else will be wherever they've got to be, but it won't be in there with me," Scott said yesterday... "I'm watching it as a fan, but also as a coach, trying to be **cognizant** of what's going on."[60]

write your own: |

Complacent

k&m-'plA-s&nt

(Adjective) content; pleased or
satisfied with how things are

Keyword: come play

Note: complaisant means "attempting or eager to please or satisfy"

The boy sat **complacent** in front of the television, refusing to **play** with the other kids.

The teacher increased the level of difficulty of his assignments because his students were too **complacent** and failed to push themselves.

She had become too **complacent**, avoiding the tough practices....[61]

It would be easy to become **complacent** about the Canadian economy given the good news this week on Canada's economic success, news that gave another boost to the Canadian dollar. But **complacency** is the last thing we can afford.[62]

write your own:

Conciliatory

k&n-'sil-y&-"tOr-E

(Adjective) attempting to unite or win over
Keyword: one silly story

Instead of fighting, the general's **conciliatory** approach is to win over his enemies by telling **one silly story**.

The union's **conciliatory** gesture broke the stalemate [standstill] and allowed the negotiations to continue on more friendly terms.

Wilson's antiwar and anti-imperialist secretary of state, William Jennings Bryan, was inclined to be **conciliatory** toward Germany in order to avoid war.[63]

Roosevelt actually pursued what amounted to a stalling strategy in Asia for months, alternating economic embargoes [trade stoppages] with **conciliatory** negotiations.[64]

write your own: _____

Concise

k&n-'sIs

(Adjective) short and clear statement/ brief
Keyword: one spice

His **concise** book on cooking told everyone that the secret to great meals was using only **one spice**.

For a timed exam, it is important to write short, **concise** answers.

As people who follow business news closely know, Coxe is no novice [beginner] to the task of explaining complex financial issues in a clear, **concise** manner.[65]

Marable, a professor at Columbia University, continues to demonstrate a mastery of polemical [disputational] writing. He is, as usual, straightforward, **concise** and adept at cutting straight to the chase.[66]

write your own:

Conspicuous

k&n-'spi-ky&-w&s

(Adjective) noticeable or obvious/
tending to attract attention
Keyword: con spit on us

When the escaped **con spit on us**, he became even more **conspicuous**.

The **conspicuous** black ink spot on his tie was noticed by nearly everyone at the meeting.

The fuel-hungry Cadillac has long been a trapping of American affluence [wealth]. It stands out even more dramatically on the pothole-rich streets of China's chaotic cities, giving members of the new moneyed class a more **conspicuous** option for flaunting [showing off] their wealth.[67]

In a courtroom crowded with defendants in blue denim and black leather, Nichola and Joseph, were **conspicuous** in their blue blazers, starched collars, and wide eyed stares.[68]

write your own:

Contumacious

"kän-tü-'mA-sh&s

(Adjective) insubordinate, rebellious, or disobedient
Keyword: cons' tune

The **cons' tune** included rebellious lyrics that sounded too **contumacious** to the prison guards.

The **contumacious** child refused to obey his parents.

You've been "conserving" calories for years—with diet sodas, low-fat milk and lately with fat-free potato chips. Yet your **contumacious** scale simply refuses to acknowledge the facts.[69]

"No," replied the captain, "but we must warn your Excellency that the island is **contumacious**."
"What do you mean?"
"That Monte Cristo, although uninhabited, yet serves occasionally as a refuge for the smugglers and pirates...." [70]

write your own: |

Corroborate

k&-'rä-b&-"rAt

(Verb) to add strength or certainty with new information
Keyword: the robber ate

Witnesses **corroborated** the charge that **the robber ate** the diamond ring.

Witnesses to the hit and run car accident **corroborated** the fact that the driver behind the wheel appeared to be drunk.

This brief encounter seemed to **corroborate** what I had sensed for several years—that Andy's death in 1987 was a hoax and that Andy is as alive as the mole on Richard Gere's back.[71]

The city released a letter … saying it has no evidence to **corroborate** the allegations or conclude that Anaheim acted improperly.[72]

write your own: _____

'krA-v&n

(Adjective) cowardly; extreme defeatism
and complete lack of resistance
Keyword: raven

The **craven raven** was too afraid to eat the food from the
boy's hand.

Given her **craven** attitude, Sue's friends were sure that she
would never go skydiving with them.

To someone who hasn't been through a decision so fraught
with conflict this must sound ridiculous, confused, irratio-
nal, and **craven**.[73]

No warrior with any concept of honor would have been so
craven.[74]

write your own: |

Credulous

'kre-j&-l&s

(Adjective) gullible; too trusting; ready to believe especially on slight or uncertain evidence
Keyword: credit [card]

The **credulous** woman handed her **credit card** to the crook who told her he needed it to make a payment on his emergency heart transplant.

Although normally quite **credulous**, Dustin refused to believe a word of what his co-workers were telling him this time.

But then it was, as we should not forget, an altogether more **credulous** age. Even the great Joseph Banks took a keen and believing interest in a series of reported sightings of mermaids off the Scottish coast at the end of the eighteenth century.[75]

"There's no demand," said ... [a] gun dealer, busily sticking "Made in USA" labels on his stock of Brazilian pistols to impress **credulous** customers from across the Saudi border.[76]

write your own:

Cryptic

'krip-tik

(Adjective) mysterious/ hard to understand/
having a hidden meaning
Keyword: crib tick

The **crib tick** left **cryptic** marks on the baby.

The pirates had a difficult time deciphering the **cryptic** marks on the treasure.

Perhaps the problem is not so much the content as his father's **cryptic** shorthand. And if it must be this incoherent scrawl [scribble that is difficult to understand], could it please be in black ink, rather than faded blue or pale brown?[77]

Wales and Ireland enjoy a curious rugby [a game similar to American football] relationship. It is far from straightforward, existing as it does in an extraordinary twilight zone of impossible and **cryptic** rituals that pertain to hardly anyone else.[78]

write your own:

62   ©Solid A, Inc.   http://SolidA.net

Cursory

'k&r-s&-rE or 'k&rs-rE

(Adjective) performed too quickly or hastily
Keyword: curse

Because Jenny was in a hurry, her **cursory** meal preparation resulted in a lot of **curses** as nothing turned out right.

The mechanic did not detect the missing spark plug during his **cursory** inspection of the vehicle.

The books of the federal government would not pass the most **cursory** audit.[79]

We are living in a very turbulent [troubled] time in which fear and instability have paralyzed everyone. A **cursory** look at the world around us would prove the reason. Every where we turn we see war, devastation and carnage [slaughter].[80]

write your own: _____

Section 2 Crossword Puzzle

Across

1. the act of breaking or state of being broken/ a gap

3. truthfulness or sincerity

4. noticeable or obvious; tending to attract attention

7. to unite, merge, or bring together into one

9. to add strength or certainty with new information

10. a harsh assortment of loud and unpleasant sounds

11. short and clear statement/ brief

15. to polish especially by rubbing

17. insubordinate, rebellious, or disobedient

18. to arrange to leave possessions, property, or money to others after death

Down

2. attempting to unite or win over

5. to punish or criticize harshly

6. having knowledge of something; informed

7. performed too quickly or hastily

8. cowardly

9. unpredictable, whimsical, or impulsive

12. gullible; too trusting

13. mysterious/ hard to understand/ having a hidden meaning

14. content; satisfied with how things are

16. to confuse or stupefy/ absorb in thought

Section 2 Multiple Choice Review

Select the word that best fits each sentence.

1. The spy took his time to wrote a _____ note using a secret code which explained where the secret weapons were hidden.
    a. cursory   b. cryptic   c. conspicuous   d. capricious

2. It was Ben's yearly responsibility to _____ his grandmother's silver before Christmas dinner.
    a. castigate   b. bequeath   c. breach   d. burnish

3. Many people _____ their estates and money to causes such as the World Wildlife Fund or the Audubon Society in their wills.
    a. corroborate   b. coalesce   c. bemuse   d. bequeath

4. A _____ glance at the letter immediately told Martha that her relationship with Joe was finished.
    a. cursory   b. craven   c. credulous   d. candor

5. As the tourists entered the jungle, they were greeted by a _____ of insect sounds.
    a. cursory   b. cacophony   c. breach   d. candor

6. With surprising _____, the teacher stated he did not know the answer.
    a. cacophony   b. conciliation   c. corroboration   d. candor

7. With Shannon's _____ tastes, her friends were never sure what to get her for her birthday.
    a. capricious   b. conspicuous   c. bemused   d. cursory

8. The _____ customer was banished from the store for her misbehavior.
    a. bemused   b. contumacious   c. burnished   d. credulous

9. An unsatisfied customer _____ the restaurant owner after discovering a dead fly in his soup.
    a. breached   b. burnished   c. corroborated   d. castigated

10. Under the pressure of the earth, plant materials _____ together over a long period of time to form oil or coal.
    a. coalesced   b. breached   c. burnished   d. bemused

11. Suzy was an easy-going, _____ child; however, she grew to be an unhappy and uncooperative teenager.
    a. craven b. complacent c. contumacious d. capricious

12. A _____ plan was drawn up to stop further conflicts between the two fighting gangs.
    a. cryptic b. conciliatory c. complacent d. capricious

13. To fit the story onto one page, Patricia had to use only _____ words.
    a. conspicuous b. concise c. conciliatory d. credulous

14. When I inquired about the incident, John's _____ look immediately indicated that he had nothing to do with what happened.
    a. cursory b. capricious c. concise d. bemused

15. No matter how hard they tried to blend in, the tourists remained _____ as a result of their dress and dialect.
    a. candor b. craven c. conspicuous d. bemused

16. Hundreds of people participated in the blind taste test and _____ the claim that more people prefer Pepsi over Coke.
    a. bequeathed b. coalesced c. corroborated d. burnished

17. Unsure of what play his opponent had in mind, Brian made a _____, but safe, move.
    a. craven b. cursory c. conspicuous d. concise

18. Cecilia was extremely _____, believing that the mythical animals in the story really exist.
    a. candor b. contumacious c. credulous d. craven

19. Sam _____ his contract when he failed to deliver the flowers to the wedding before the ceremony.
    a. bemused b. corroborated c. breached d. bequeathed

20. It is often wondered, with all the people that receive traffic tickets, if they are _____ of all the traffic laws.
    a. credulous b. cognizant c. conspicuous d. complacent

Section 2 Matching Review

Match the word on the left to the correct meaning on the right.

1. _____ Bemuse		**A.** cowardly
2. _____ Bequeath		**B.** attempting to unite or win over
3. _____ Breach		**C.** gullible; too trusting
4. _____ Burnish		**D.** short and clear statement/brief
5. _____ Cacophony		**E.** to unite, merge, or bring together into one
6. _____ Candor		**F.** to add strength or certainty with new information
7. _____ Capricious		**G.** a harsh assortment of loud and unpleasant sounds
8. _____ Castigate		**H.** the act of breaking or state of being broken/ a gap
9. _____ Coalesce		**I.** to punish or criticize harshly
10. _____ Cognizant		**J.** having knowledge of something; informed
11. _____ Complacent		**K.** unpredictable, whimsical, or impulsive
12. _____ Conciliatory		**L.** insubordinate, rebellious, or disobedient
13. _____ Concise		**M.** mysterious/ hard to understand/ having a hidden meaning
14. _____ Conspicuous		**N.** performed too quickly or hastily
15. _____ Contumacious		**O.** to confuse or stupefy/ absorb in thought
16. _____ Corroborate		**P.** content; satisified with how things are
17. _____ Craven		**Q.** to arrange to leave possessions, property, or money to others after death
18. _____ Credulous		**R.** to polish especially by rubbing
19. _____ Cryptic		**S.** truthfulness or sincerity
20. _____ Cursory		**T.** noticeable or obvious; tending to attract attention

Section Three

Debilitate

di-'bi-l&-"tAt

(Verb) to weaken or lessen the strength
of someone or something
Keyword: the bill he ate

The ink on **the bill he ate** had a **debilitating** affect on his body.

The disease **debilitated** the dog and left her crippled.

Great blunders on great stages often haunt the minds and **debilitate** the play of famous golfers the rest of their careers.[81]

She has no resources or support system to help when she misses work because of complications from her painful and **debilitating** illness.[82]

write your own:

Debunk

dE-'b&[ng]k

(Verb) to show that something is not as genuine or good as it appears
Keyword: top bunk

".. SO IT'S NOT TRUE. WILL YOU SLEEP HERE NOW?"

YES!

After the camp counselor **debunked** the myth that some-one died in the **top bunk**, the campers were willing to sleep there.

The scientist worked to **debunk** the myth that a monster lived in the lake.

The study ... **debunked** assumptions that the bear population was booming [rising]. Instead, it found bears were moving from the mountains to neighborhoods, leading to increased conflicts and more bear deaths.[83]

[He] **debunks** certain myths, like the assumption that a bachelor's degree is prohibitively [exorbitantly] expensive, and he upholds other notions about what it takes to get into college.[84]

write your own: _____

Deflate

di-'flAt

(Verb) to reduce in size or importance/ to let the air out

Keyword: the flake

When **the Flake** truck became stuck under the low bridge, the truck driver's ego was **deflated** as he had to deflate the tires to dislodge it.

The comedian felt **deflated** when no one laughed at her jokes.

Humiliating performance in sports **deflates** self-esteem the way a sharp nail in your driveway leads to a flat tire, especially in a kid whose report card also leaves a whole lot to be desired.[85]

Headline: The future of space? Will the next generation's waning [decreasing] interest in being astronauts **deflate** support for space programs?[86]

write your own: |

                                    http://SolidA.net

Deleterious

"de-l&-'ti-rE-&s

(Adjective) harmful or detrimental
Keyword: delete

With **deleterious** intent, the man **deleted** all the files on his company's computer after being fired.

It has been proven that smoking is **deleterious** to not only the smoker's health, but to those nearby who breathe in the smoke.

Likewise, there is no conclusive evidence linking **deleterious** human health effects to trace pesticide residues in the food supply.[87]

Although abstinence is obviously the safest course and is now advised by most doctors and public health officials, the fact is that we still do not know whether modest [a little] alcohol consumption has any **deleterious** effects on the fetus.[88]

write your own:

Demeanor

(Noun) a way of behaving towards others; disposition

Keyword: meaner

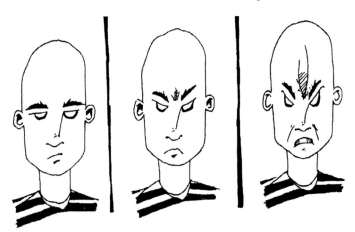

In a short period of time, the criminal's **demeanor** became **meaner** and meaner.

The **demeanor** on the judge's face communicated to the delinquent boys that they were in serious trouble.

Gervin, 51, won four NBA scoring titles with the Spurs and earned the moniker [nickname] "Iceman" for his on-court **demeanor**.[89]

The solemn [grave] **demeanor** of a monk from Thame Monastery belies [falsely represents] some of the lighter moods of Mani Rimdu, an annual festival of drama and dance to banish evil spirits.[90]

write your own: |

Denigration

"de-ni-'grA-sh&n

(Noun) the act of making something
seem not good or important
Keyword: demonstration

The audience showed increasing **denigration** for the
magician's **demonstrations** because his tricks looked fake.

Sarah was put down and **denigrated** by others for having different political beliefs.

When you degrade, scold, or criticize yourself, you are out of
alignment with the greater part of yourself, and there are no
greater crippling thoughts than those of self-**denigration**.[91]

Columnist Andrew Bolt told the Victorian Supreme Court he
didn't wage a campaign of **denigration** against [the] deputy
chief magistrate [judge] ... but reported matters in the public
interest when he criticized the court's "undue leniency [toler-
ance]." [92]

write your own: |

Denunciation

di-"n&nt-sE-'A-sh&n

(Noun) public accusation or disapproval
Keyword: the nuns'creation

After unveiling the statue, the angry priest's **denunciation** of the **nuns' creation** was publicly known to everyone.

The principal's **denunciation** of cheating is backed up by a minimum punishment of a week-long expulsion.

Union president Donald Fehr issued a terse **denunciation** and then filed a grievance [complaint].[93]

While Elliott was wrapping up the meeting with another **denunciation** of the [program], Levitt was getting a friendlier reception out in the hallway.[94]

write your own: |

Derision

di-'ri-zh&n

(Noun) ridicule or disrespect
Keyword: division

The student's inability to do **division** caused his classmates to treat him with **derision**.

Stuart faced **derision** at school because his classmates disapproved of his disruptive behavior.

As discussed throughout, verbal and physical **derision** or abuse in school should be considered a form of criminal behavior and punished accordingly. Peer cruelty is unacceptable and a clear violation of kids' rights.[95]

[He] did not want to be an object of **derision**; it was bad for discipline - and it was worse for discipline if the men shared some secret unknown to their officers.[96]

write your own: |

'de-si-"krAt

(Verb) to show a lack of respect towards or to violate
(especially something holy)
Keyword: desert crate

The tomb robbers **desecrated** the **desert crates** by lighting them on fire.

The female tourists **desecrated** the Muslim mosque by not covering their heads before entering.

Lloyd remains active in the campaign to get a constitutional amendment to make it illegal to **desecrate** the flag....[97]

Environmental groups have led a campaign against the development. It would wreck one of the last havens [refuge] of biodiversity near Athens and it would **desecrate** a historic site where democracy won against overwhelming odds.[98]

write **own:**
your

Deter

di-'t&r

(Verb) to discourage or prevent
Keyword: detour

After making an unexpected **detour** on the safari, the guide **deterred** the tourists from getting out of the bus to prevent them from being eaten by a hungry animal.

Airport screeners **deterred** the passengers from boarding the plane with illegal items as they meticulously inspected their luggage.

My own judgment would come down against imprisoning someone for life in order to **deter** him from self-destructive behavior....[99]

A plan to protect fossil sites has been stalled by worries it could **deter** amateur paleontologists [scientists who study life from fossil remains] and stifle [deter] growth in rapidly developing east Hillsborough County.[100]

write your own: _____

Devious

'dE-vE-&s

(Adjective) sly; not straightforward
Keyword: TV bus

The **devious** reporters on the **TV bus** led the public to believe that the earthquake was disastrous by filming the only building that was damaged.

In order for his business to succeed, he developed a **devious** scheme to close down his competitors.

He was aggressive, he was abusive ... and he was a **devious** politician who was quite unscrupulous [without moral integrity] in the methods he used to bring down his enemies.[101]

And in the last several weeks this **devious** microscopic organism apparently unleashed another nasty attack, killing tens of thousands of fish in a 4.5-mile stretch of Maryland's Pocomoke River....[102]

write your own:

©Solid A, Inc.   http://SolidA.net

Didactic

dI-'dak-tik

(Adjective) intended to be educational and informational/ aimed to teach a moral lesson
Keyword: died in the attic

A rat **died in the attic** as a result of listening to the long, boring, **didactic** lecture.

The church sponsored a **didactic** play designed to teach moral principles to the teenage audience.

It is history as it should be: entertaining without being glib [superficial], informative without being **didactic**.[103]

Organizers want that message—that we increase our awareness about the world around us and maybe even turn concern into action—to be delivered through a wide selection of films they say are not **didactic** or preachy but engaging and enlightening.[104]

write your own: |

Diminution

"di-m&-'nü-sh&n
(Noun) a decrease in size
Keyword: ammunition

The **diminution** of water caused by the drought, led to a shortage of **ammunition** for the squirt guns.

The **diminution** of ice-skating talent in recent years consequently led to a decrease in spectators.

Thomas Merton, the great theologian, tells us "in order to realize himself, man has to risk the **diminution** and even the total loss of all his reality in favor of another, for if any man would have his life, he must lose it."[105]

The Earth's magnetic field has diminished by perhaps as much as 6 % in the last century. Any **diminution** in magnetism is likely to be bad news, because magnetism, apart from holding notes to refrigerators and keeping our compasses pointing to the right way, plays a vital role in keeping us alive.[106]

write your own: |

Discursive

dis-'k&r-siv

(Adjective) changing topics
Keyword: curves

The teacher described a **discursive** essay as being a bad road with many **curves**, rambling in all directions.

In an attempt to steer the audience's questions away from the sensitive subject, the governor gave **discursive** answers to their inquiries.

While the movie's producers may have been trying to streamline Kerr's **discursive** collection of essays into a standard-issue Hollywood plotline, the result completely misses the point of Kerr's work....[107]

As such it has the **discursive** character of a diary, rather than the ordered structure of a more formally constructed piece.[108]

write your own: |

Disdain

dis-'dAn

(Noun) a strong dislike for someone
or something; contempt
(Verb) to dislike someone or something strongly
Keyword: dish drain

After doing poorly, Jim had such **disdain** for his test results that he crumpled it up and sent it down the **dish drain.**

Rallying around the fur store's entrance with picket signs, the
group showed outright **disdain** for the killing of animals to
make coats.

Indeed, he has shown little or no respect for the jury's verdict.
Rather, he has displayed an attitude of contempt and **disdain** for the jury's verdict....[109]

I have heard that she made no secret of her **disdain** for his
appearance.[110]

write own: |

©Solid A, Inc.   http://SolidA.net

Dismantle

(Verb) to take apart or disassemble
Keyword: this handle

After taking out the bolts, **this handle** was **dismantled**.

In the final football game of the season, the Capital Cougars **dismantled** the Shelton Highclimber's defense and easily won the game.

At its height [the British Empire] it had covered a quarter of the world's land surface and governed around the same proportion of its population. It took just three decades to **dismantle**, leaving only a few scattered islands....[111]

[He] contends that the city needs more officers if it is to reduce homicides, **dismantle** gangs and make Los Angeles safer.[112]

write your own:

Disparage

(Verb) to criticize, degrade, or belittle
Keyword: the spare

Stuck in the middle of nowhere with a flat tire, he **disparaged** his friend for forgetting to replace **the spare.**

The governor's unpopular plan to raise taxes was **disparaged** in newspapers across the state.

I don't want to **disparage** mammography [procedure to detect breast cancer]; it is still the best detection tool we have right now. But by the time we can see a cancer, whether by mammography, ultrasound or MRI, it's often too far along.[113]

His rivalrous [given to conflict] anger is now directed away from the father, and towards himself. The boy is less prone to **disparage** the father, more prone to censure [criticize] himself....[114]

write your own: |

Disperse

di-'sp&rs

(Verb) to scatter or break up
Keyword: purse

The thief grabbed her **purse**, **dispersing** all of its contents on the road.

The wedding party quickly **dispersed** when it started to rain.

The Somerville initiative would allow police to arrest suspected gang members who loiter and do not **disperse** after three hours.[115]

For best results, use bread machine yeast. Its finer granulation helps the yeast **disperse** more thoroughly during mixing and kneading.[116]

write own:
your

Dogmatic

dog-'ma-tik

(Adjective) being certain that one is right;
highly opinionated; authoritative
Keyword: dog mat

We should have warned the mailman that our dog Rufus is very **dogmatic** about who he will allow to step on his **dog mat**.

The religious organization was **dogmatic** and forceful in its beliefs.

Deeply spiritual, but never annoyingly **dogmatic**, she fixated on serving God in a professional capacity.[117]

They're very rigid and **dogmatic** about what the business needs to look like....[118]

write your own: |

                    http://SolidA.net

Dulcet

'd&l-s&t

(Adjective) pleasing to listen to; soothing
Keyword: dull set

Everyone thinks my grandma has a **dull set** of records. However, she considers the music **dulcet**, claiming it has a soothing and calming quality.

I couldn't decide which was more relaxing during my massage; the massage itself or the **dulcet** music playing in the background.

Peters's voice is one of the great instruments in the world of musical theatre—**dulcet** but full of attack, slightly mournful around the edges.[119]

They manage to argue in **dulcet** tones for the remainder of the meal while Sima and I exchanged wan [gloomy] smiles across the table.[120]

write your own:

Section 3 Crossword Puzzle

Across

3. to criticize, degrade, or belittle

5. to discourage or prevent

6. a decrease in size

7. pleasing to listen to; soothing

8. sly; not straightforward

14. to show a lack of respect towards something; to violate (especially something holy)

16. to weaken or lessen the strength of someone or something

17. public accusation or disapproval

Down

1. being certain that one is right; highly opinionated; authoritative

2. the act of making something seem not good or important

3. to take apart or disassemble

4. changing topics

6. to reduce in size or importance/ to let the air out

8. to scatter or break up

9. harmful or detrimental

10. ridicule, disrespect

11. a way of behaving towards others; disposition

12. intended to be educational and informational

13. to show that something is not as genuine or good as it appears

15. a strong dislike for someone or something; contempt

Section 3 Multiple Choice Review

Select the word that best fits each sentence.

1. Part of what made the hypnotist so powerful was his _____ voice that lulled people into a deep sleep.
   a. didactic   b. discursive   c. dulcet   d. disdainful

2. Josh finally decided to quit his job because he could no longer take the constant _____ from his co-workers.
   a. desecration   b. diminution   c. denigration   d. deflation

3. The new teacher attempted to _____ the rumor that she was mean and a hard grader by going out of her way to show kindness to the students.
   a. disperse   b. debunk   c. debilitate   d. deter

4. The logging industry has been very _____ to rain forests.
   a. deleterious   b. didactic   c. discursive   d. devious

5. Jackie could hardly stand to listen to her father's long _____ on rock music.
   a. dogma   b. denunciation   c. derision   d. dulcet

6. To let the management know they did not like the new employment policies, the employees shouted hoots of _____ after it was read.
   a. derision   b. denigration   c. demeanor   d. denunciation

7. Unknowingly, the young boy _____ the holy fountain of the church by washing his hands in the water.
   a. deterred   b. desecrated   c. dismantled   d. deflated

8. While classes were closed, teachers attended a workshop designed to change the way they taught from a traditional _____ approach to a more discovery-based approach.
   a. didactic   b. discursive   c. deleterious   d. disparaging

9. Japan _____ the U.S. naval fleet in its surprise attack on Pearl Harbor.
   a. debilitated   b. disparaged   c. desecrated   d. debunked

10. The boy played a _____ prank on his teacher by moving the hour hand forward one hour on the classroom clock.
a. didactic   b. discursive   c. dulcet   d. devious

11. Jennifer exudes a carefree _____; instead of walking to class she skips.
a. denigration   b. derision   c. demeanor   d. diminution

12. The mother attempted to _____ her children from fighting by threatening to spank them.
a. debilitate   b. desecrate   c. deter   d. denigrate

13. The barn had to be _____ before a house could be built on the same location.
a. dismantled   b. debilitated   c. dispersed   d. deflated

14. The girl's _____ insistence that Zaire was located in Central America proved to be wrong.
a. discursive   b. deleterious   c. dogmatic   d. dulcet

15. One can achieve a _____ of stress by a regiment of cardiovascular exercise.
a. derision   b. denunciation   c. diminution   d. demeanor

16. Though the student was eager to partake in the English composition class, his first paper received a bad grade due to its incoherent thesis statement and its _____ organization.
a. discursive   b. didactic   c. devious   d. deflated

17. As the wind blows, dandelion seeds are _____ into the air.
a. disparaged   b. dispersed   c. desecrated   d. dismantled

18. Most country music fans in the city _____ the new rock radio station that replaced their prominent country station.
a. deflate   b. disdain   c. deters   d. debunk

19. Michael Jordan helped _____ the Knicks, by scoring over fifty points.
a. disdain   b. debunk   c. disperse   d. deflate

20. After the company went bankrupt, both the workers and the public immediately _____ the CEO and the president with a harsh article about their incompetence in the newspaper.
a. disparaged   b. debunked   c. deterred   d. dismantled

Section 3 Matching Review

Match the word on the left to the correct meaning on the right.

1. _____ Debilitate

2. _____ Debunk

3. _____ Deflate

4. _____ Deleterious

5. _____ Demeanor

6. _____ Denigration

7. _____ Denunciation

8. _____ Derision

9. _____ Desecrate

10. _____ Deter

11. _____ Devious

12. _____ Didactic

13. _____ Diminution

14. _____ Discursive

15. _____ Disdain

16. _____ Dismantle

17. _____ Disparage

18. _____ Disperse

19. _____ Dogmatic

20. _____ Dulcet

A. to discourage or prevent
B. ridicule or disrespect
C. to weaken or lessen the strength of someone or something
D. to criticize, degrade, or belittle
E. sly; not straightforward
F. to reduce in size or importance; to let the air out
G. changing topics
H. being certain that one is right; highly opinionated; authoritative
I. public accusation or disapproval
J. to scatter or break up
K. a decrease in size
L. a strong dislike for someone or something; contempt
M. to show that something is not as genuine or good as it appears
N. to take apart or disassemble
O. a way of behaving towards others; disposition
P. harmful or detrimental
Q. pleasing to listen to; soothing
R. to show a lack of respect towards or to violate (especially something holy)
S. intended to be educational and informational
T. the act of making something seem not good or important

Section Four

Duplicity

du-'pli-s&-tE or dyu-'pli-s&-tE

(Noun) deception, dishonesty, or double-dealing

Keyword: Duplex City

In his **duplicity**, the realtor tricked the two families into buying the same home in **Duplex City**.

The double agent went to prison after his **duplicity** in spying was discovered.

There was an element of **duplicity** in Wilson's dealings here.[121]

Perhaps the greatest contradiction in [Mr.] Pound is that as clearly as he sees the **duplicity** and corruption in the so-called movement, he still trusts in it.[122]

write your own: |

Ebb

'eb

(Verb) to decrease or decline slowly
Keyword: web

The spider **web** slowly **ebbed** away with the wind and rain.

The crowd at the swimming pool slowly **ebbed** as the children started leaving for dinner.

The owner of Killeen House Hotel in Killarney is witnessing his tourist season **ebb** away before it has even started.[123]

That was enough to put a foot and a half of water in the famous square—the lowest point in Venice—but it was nothing historic. What happened next was historic. Whipped up by sirocco winds that blew ceaselessly [constantly] up the Adriatic [Sea], the tide refused to **ebb**.[124]

write your own: |

i-'fAs or e-'fAs

(Verb) to erase, to wipe out, or vanish

Keyword: erase

The student nearly panicked when the teacher **effaced** the homework assignment from the blackboard, and **erased** it before the pupil could write it down.

The statue was **effaced** by the constant exposure to wind and rain until it was no longer recognizable.

Online communication cannot **efface** face-to-face contact.[125]

Jarrell's poem "Burning the Letters" has great power. The wife of a pilot shot down over the Pacific tries to **efface** the painful memory by burning his letters to her.[126]

write **own:** your

Effluvia

e-'flü-vE-&

(Noun) a toxic odor or vapor
Note: Effluvium is singular
Keyword: flu

The **effluvia** from the science lab resulted in a **flu** epidemic at school.

Specialists were brought into the home that was suspected to have noxious leaks of **effluvia** circulating in the air.

This is the time of year when many of us survey the maze of critics' "top 10" lists and respond, in the mode of John McEnroe, "You can't be serious." How could anyone conjure up such a mixed bag of cinematic [related to motion pictures] **effluvia**?[127]

Soviet industrial projects account for many of the detonations [explosions], which, along with [nuclear] reactor **effluvia**, have deposited most of the world's nuclear waste in the region, including at least six reactors dumped off the coast.[128]

write your own:

Effrontery

i-'fr&n-t&-rE or e-'fr&n-t&-rE

(Noun) boldness, nerve, or courage
Keyword: in front of me

As the king gave Arthur a medal of honor he said, "This man showed great **effrontery** by standing **in front of me** during the battle."

With **effrontery**, the student spoke in his graduation speech about changes that needed to be made to the school administration.

Book Title: Samuel Johnson's Book of Insults: A Compendium of Snubs, Sneers, Slights and **Effronteries** from the 18th Century's Master.[129]

Just between ourselves, I continually wonder at my own **effrontery** in opposing this young man who's going to do so much for us all.[130]

write your own: |

          http://SolidA.net

Embellish

im-'be-lish

(Verb) to make beautiful or interesting by adding something/ to add false details
Keyword: bell

The **bell** was **embellished** with decorations to commemorate the 4th of July.

Rudy **embellished** the story of the accident so much that he made himself sound like the hero.

It's a bold man who sets out not only to retell one of the most beloved adventures in American history, but also to **embellish** it and make it his own.[131]

The part of the garment you **embellish** should be at a flattering place on your body. Don't **embellish** hemlines that fall at areas you would prefer to de-emphasize, such as the hips or the thighs.[132]

write your own:

im-'pir-i-k&l

(Adjective) based on what is experienced or observed
Keyword: empire

The billionaire's **empire** was built on **empirical** data of experience and observations of the stock market.

The students learned how to record **empirical** data they gathered in science class.

Art is not the best medium for representing **empirical** data, as the artist, by definition, has a big hand in any outcome.[133]

But all this is speculation. Nobody has a shred of **empirical** evidence that any of these influences actually boost IQ (Intelligence Quotient).[134]

write your own: |

Engender

in-'jen-d&r or en-'jen-d&r

(Verb) to cause something to occur or develop
Keyword: engine

Larry's powerful **engine** helped him **engender** victory in the car race.

Her angry words against the policeman **engendered** his wrath against her, and consequently she was given a very expensive ticket.

In addition to the bad feelings such court battles **engender**, fighting over possessions gets expensive.[135]

It's one thing for you to **engender** customer loyalty—but what about regaining the loyalty of customers you've already lost?[136]

write your own: _____

Ephemeral

i-'fem-r&l or i-'fEm-r&l

(Adjective) fleeting, short lived, or transitory
Keyword: emeralds

Susan's engagement was **ephemeral** after discovering that her **emerald** ring was made of plastic.

The song had **ephemeral** success on the radio, and was taken off the air shortly after its debut since it offended many people.

A close [completion of a business agreement] that you get by following Technique 14 is likely to be both artificial and **ephemeral**. Because it's built on trickery, it can never bring you the sustained business that every professional wants.[137]

All human life is likened to evening dew and morning frost, considered something quite fragile and **ephemeral**.[138]

write your own: |

©Solid A, Inc. http://SolidA.net

Epitome

i-'pi-t&-mE

(Noun) a part that represents the whole/ perfect example of something/ summary

Keyword: pits for me

Out of all of my workers, John is the **epitome** of an ideal construction worker, digging hundreds of **pits for me**.

The training session was the **epitome** of what the job would be like, and helped him determine if he would like the job.

Breuer was the **epitome** of the family doctor; he made house calls and would see patients as early as 6:30 a.m.[139]

In the United States, models and actresses are held up as the **epitome** of beauty, yet these women who grace the covers of magazines and star in films know that their careers would be cut short if they didn't protect their most precious asset—their skin.[140]

write your own:

Equivocal

i-'kwi-v&-k&l

(Adjective) subject to multiple interpretations;
questionable; ambiguous
Keyword: quiver

As the judge's ruling was **equivocal**, the convict imagined the worst and began to **quiver**, not understanding the ambiguous nature of his sentence.

The detective's responses were purposely **equivocal** so the public would remain unaware until an official report was released.

Evidence for true cannibalism among dinosaurs is **equivocal**. ... Analyses of chewed bones suggest that tyrannosaurs often ate tyrannosaurs, but the teeth marks aren't distinctive enough to determine whether victim and predator were members of the same species.[141]

Nothing is more **equivocal**. There are guilty men who can hide a true crime ... and innocent victims who confess to crimes of which they were not guilty.[142]

write your own:

    http://SolidA.net

Esoteric

"e-s&-'ter-ik or "e-s&-'te-rik

(Adjective) understood by very few people/
strange or unusual
Keyword: S.O.S.

On the video, the prisoner of war used his eyes to blink an
esoteric S.O.S. while being forced to make a false statement that he was being treated well.

Her strange and **esoteric** taste in clothes was appreciated by
very few people who knew her.

Consider this description of the job from a critic at a midsize
daily: "Unlike movie critics or drama critics, [art critics] regularly deal with **esoteric** and obscure art forms that the average newspaper reader might find baffling."[143]

Bruce Thompson holds one of Maryland government's more
esoteric jobs—assistant state underwater archaeologist....[144]

write your own: _____

Euphoric

yu-'for-ik or yu-'fOr-ik

(Adjective) feeling well and happy; feeling of elation
Keyword: "U fork"

The archaeologist was **euphoric** to discover the first "**U fork**" ever found.

Bonita was in a **euphoric** mood for weeks planning her dream vacation in the Caribbean.

Belli describes the **euphoric** victory celebrations as if under a magical spell.[145]

The new law sets a maximum fine of $100 for "medical marijuana" users who have less than an ounce of the leaf. It makes Maryland the 10th state since 1996 to ease or eliminate sanctions for medical use of the herb, which gained wide use during the 1960s because of its **euphoric** effects.[146]

write your own:

Evince

i-'vints or i-'vins

(Verb) to show or manifest in an obvious way. to display clearly; reveal
Keyword: evidence

The **evidence evinced** to everyone that John was responsible for tracking in the mud.

It was strange to learn that Traci enjoys canoeing so much as she has always **evinced** a fear of water.

"Do you have any questions for me?" There was a long silence, and the head of the school was acutely uncomfortable, fearing that no boy would **evince** any interest at all and the school would be embarrassed.[147]

"The canoes," [Meriwether] Louis wrote on February 22, "along with the woodwork and sculpture of these people (Native Americans) as well as these hats and their waterproof baskets **evince** ingenuity common among the Aborigines of America."[148]

write your own:

Exculpate

'ek-sk&l-"pAt

(Verb) to clear from a charge of guilt or fault

Keyword: X skull

The pirate was **exculpated** and released after it was discovered that he was not responsible for vandalizing the ship with the "**X skull**" spray painting.

The defendant was **exculpated** of all charges after the real culprit was discovered.

Should you draw the death penalty in this state, you have thirty days to find any evidence that would **exculpate** you.[149]

Leppo quickly moved to have the charges thrown out on the basis of the detective's contradictory testimony and on the grounds that the lost evidence might help **exculpate** his client.[150]

write your own:

Expedient

ik-'spE-dE-&nt

(Adjective) helpful or useful in a certain situation/ serving one's self interest

Keyword: speedy ants

When you need to make an ant hill, it is **expedient** to have **speedy ants**.

The city's decision to purchase larger garbage trucks instead of promoting recycling was an **expedient** solution to the increase of trash in the city, a decision they would eventually regret.

He is much like [President] Clinton, with whom he shared a particular closeness even when it was not politically **expedient**.[151]

Available land appeared endless, therefore, when the old soil became exhausted ... most colonists found it far more **expedient** to burn trees to clear new acreage than to do the painstaking work of maintaining the fertility of established fields.[152]

write your own:

Extenuating/Extenuate

ik-'sten-y&-"wAt-ng

(Verb) to lessen the seriousness; make less
blameworthy; excusing

*Extenuating is a verb that functions as an adjective

Keyword: exterminating

STOP! THOSE ARE THE LAST BUGS!

Due to **extenuating** circumstances, **exterminating** the
bugs was put to a quick stop after it was discovered that the
bugs were endangered.

Rick did not care about any **extenuating** conditions that surrounded the car accident; he was going to be mad regardless
as a result of the damage to his car.

No matter how **extenuating** the circumstances, no one else
gets the blame if the plows are too slow. Snow removal can
make or break a political career.[153]

Assuredly, Madame, you are determined to **extenuate** certain things and exaggerate others.[154]

write your own: |

Extol

ik-'stOl

(Verb) to praise highly
Keyword: toll

At the **toll**, the attendant stopped to admire and **extol** my car.

Tired of listening to June and Bob **extol** the intelligence and talents of their children for hours on end, their friends now avoid them.

I **extol** the joys of being a father every chance I get. Having changed diapers, given baths, fed, clothed and cuddled, I can say with authority that it is indeed a wonderful experience.[155]

You probably have heard the statement that "It takes thirty-five miles of walking to lose a pound of fat." Weight-control experts who remind you of this fact then go on to **extol** the virtues of their particular diet.[156]

write your own:

ek-'strA-nE-&s

(Adjective) irrelevant, unrelated, or unnecessary
Keyword: neck strain

The jury ruled that the man's purported **neck strain** was an **extraneous** issue in the car accident after they learned that he had just won the New York City Marathon with the "injury."

Not having time for any **extraneous** questions, the President focused only on the questions dealing with the situation at hand.

[When taking pictures with your camera] zoom in on your item: Don't leave a bunch of **extraneous** background in your pictures. Crop out extra background in your pictures.[157]

He began to cut away all **extraneous** detail, to write only in dramatic scenes....[158]

write your own: |

Fatuous

'fa-chü-&s or 'fa-tyü-&s

(Adjective) stupid; lacking good sense; foolish or silly
Keyword: fat

The **fat** hog was known for upsetting the other farm animals with his **fatuous** remarks.

Her **fatuous** suggestions about how the reception should be run was unbelievably stupid and in bad taste.

A lot of the trendy stuff is really just **fatuous** nonsense....[159]

The Kenyans are to distance running what the Yankees once were to baseball: so infuriatingly good that even aspiring to beat them seems to be an act of **fatuous** optimism.[160]

write your own: |

Section 4 Crossword Puzzle

©Solid A, Inc.   http://SolidA.net

Across

1. a part that represents the whole/ perfect example of something/ summary

3. to erase, to wipe out, or vanish

4. subject to multiple interpretations; questionable; ambiguous

8. to decrease or decline slowly

9. feeling well and happy

10. to clear from a charge of guilt or fault

12. stupid; lacking good sense

14. to cause something to occur or develop

16. to lessen the seriousness; make less blameworthy; excusing

17. to show or manifest in an obvious way

Down

1. a toxic odor or vapor

2. to praise highly

4. based on what is experienced or observed

5. understood by very few people/ strange or unusual

6. deception, dishonesty, or double-dealing

7. to make beautiful or interesting by adding something/ to add false details

11. boldness, nerve, or courage

13. irrelevant, unrelated, or unnecessary

14. helpful or useful in a certain situation/serving one's self interest

15. fleeting, short lived, or transitory

Section 4 Multiple Choice Review

Select the word that best fits each sentence.

1. Joseph's bad day on Friday was the _____ of his whole week.
    a. ephemeral   b. effluvia   c. duplicity   d. epitome

2. Other than using _____ terms, Chris could find no other positive way to describe the view from the top of the mountain.
    a. euphoric   b. equivocal   c. ephemera   d. extraneous

3. Because of his _____ when dealing with others, Robert lost two of his closest friends when they discovered he lied to them.
    a. effluvia   b. epitome   c. effrontery   d. duplicity

4. After scoring the winning goal, Roberto was _____ as the school hero.
    a. extolled   b. ebbed   c. evinced   d. exculpated

5. The waiter was so angered by the _____ of his customer, that he switched tables with his co-worker.
    a. effrontery   b. epitome   c. embellishment   d. exculpation

6. The bride's dress was _____ with sequins and beads.
    a. engendered   b. effaced   c. ebbed   d. embellished

7. Periods of peace-time often _____ advances in the arts, architecture and literature.
    a. extenuate   b. engender   c. efface   d. exculpate

8. The teacher was frustrated when she called on a student, who was obviously not paying attention. His _____ answer made the whole class laugh.
    a. extraneous   b. empirical   c. fatuous   d. ephemeral

9. Lila left out any _____ circumstances when describing the evening to her mother so that she would not get into trouble.
    a. fatuous   b. equivocal   c. extenuating   d. euphoric

10. The children's excitement about swimming was _____ because it started to rain just after they left for the pool.
    a. ephemeral   b. duplicity   c. fatuous   d. expedient

11. No one completely understood the movie star's many _____ statements on the TV talk show.
    a. empirical   b. extraneous   c. equivocal   d. euphoric

12. Unable to appreciate or understand their brother's strange fetish for cereal boxes, Lance's collection remained _____.
    a. fatuous   b. esoteric   c. extraneous   d. expedient

13. Because his students _____ a love for the outdoors, the teacher held class outside.
    a. engendered   b. evinced   c. extenuated   d. embellished

14. The child was _____ when his older brother stepped forward and admitted guilt to the broken mirror.
    a. effaced   b. evinced   c. extolled   d. exculpated

15. Students were warned to be cautious of _____ while conducting science experiments.
    a. duplicity   b. effluvia   c. euphoric   d. effrontery

16. Placing cameras in the hallways appeared to be an _____ solution for stopping bullying and fighting in school, but it could not eliminate verbal threats by students.
    a. exculpated   b. esoteric   c. equivocal   d. expedient

17. The _____ data was/were not entirely reliable. More research would be required before the product could be made available to the public.
    a. ephemeral   b. esoteric   c. empirical   d. exculpated

18. Because she waited too long to apply for a job, all of the best work opportunities _____ away.
    a. engendered   b. embellished   c. evinced   d. ebbed

19. The teacher was forced to weed through a lot of _____ information to get to the main points of the student's paper.
    a. expedient   b. extraneous   c. extenuating   d. fatuous

20. Local police tried to _____ auto theft by inserting tracking devices in every car in the city.
    a. evince   b. exculpate   c. efface   d. extol

Section 4 Matching Review

Match the word on the left to the correct meaning on the right.

1. _____ Duplicity

2. _____ Ebb

3. _____ Efface

4. _____ Effluvia

5. _____ Effrontery

6. _____ Embellish

7. _____ Empirical

8. _____ Engender

9. _____ Ephemeral

10. _____ Epitome

11. _____ Equivocal

12. _____ Esoteric

13. _____ Euphoric

14. _____ Evince

15. _____ Exculpate

16. _____ Expedient

17. _____ Extenuate

18. _____ Extol

19. _____ Extraneous

20. _____ Fatuous

A. to decrease or decline slowly

B. irrelevant, unrelated, or unnecessary

C. boldness, nerve, or courage

D. to make beautiful or interesting by adding something/to add false details

E. helpful or useful in a certain situation/ serving one's self interest

F. based on what is experienced or observed

G. fleeting, short live, or transitory

H. deception, dishonesty, or double-dealing

I. to show or manifest in an obvious way

J. to erase, to wipe out, or vanish

K. to lessen the seriousness; make less blameworthy; excusing

L. to praise highly

M. subject to multiple interpretations; questionable; ambiguous

N. to clear from a charge of guilt or fault

O. to cause something to occur or develop

P. feeling well and happy

Q. a part that represents the whole/ perfect example of something/ summary

R. stupid; lacking good sense

S. understood by very few people/ strange or unusual

T. a toxic odor or vapor

Section Five

Fitful

'fit-f&l

(Adjective) irregular; occurring in spurts
Keyword: fist full

His first time milking cows with a **fist full** of udder produced a **fitful** stream of milk.

The baby's shallow, **fitful** breathing during the night further alarmed the worried parents.

I believe that in infants and young children a cause-and-effect relationship exists between disturbed sleep and **fitful**, fussy behaviors.[161]

During her long first night in the Rackham house, during a sleep that's tainted [spoiled] by the **fitful** barking of a distant dog, Sugar dreams all sorts of [strange] things.[162]

write your own: |

Florid

'flor-&d or 'flär-&d

(Adjective) having too much decoration; gaudy/
flushed; tinged with red
Keyword: floral

The **floral** hat, decorated with gaudy looking flowers, was
far too **florid** to wear to the party.

The interior designer had a habit of over-decorating and consequently became well known for the **florid** rooms she created.

The little man tugged an enormous suitcase out onto the porch,
never taking notice of me, his **florid** face streaked with per-
spiration.[163]

In a minute, a short man with a **florid** face and bald head
came out of the office with quick, hurried steps, like a mouse
running from a hole in the wall.[164]

write your own: _____

Flout

'flaut

(Verb) to disregard or disobey intentionally
Keyword: trout

The **trout flouted** the sign and decided to swim wherever he wished.

At the end of the last day of school, the group of rowdy students decided to **flout** the school rules and race down the hall, making as much noise as possible.

The independent television commission said that if YOU TV continued to **flout** its codes of practice, it would consider taking the channel off air.[165]

From a Yankee perspective, these laws may seem unjust. But is that sufficient reason to **flout** them?[166]

write your own: |

     http://SolidA.net

Forlorn

f&r-'lorn or for-'lorn

(Adjective) nearly hopeless; deserted; sad and lonely due to isolation

Keyword: four horns

The small rhino with **four horns** felt **forlorn** and lonely because he was different.

The **forlorn** and forgotten garden was overgrown with weeds.

Choked for sunlight, the **forlorn** chocolate trees at Garfield Park Conservancy produced few of the cocoa beans used to make chocolate.[167]

For years, some zoos have facilitated elephant courtship by loading a female onto a truck, driving her to a breeding bull and hoping for the best. The hope was usually **forlorn**. Infertility [inability to become pregnant] is a problem.[168]

write your own:

Frenetic

fri-'ne-tik

(Adjective) frantic, wildly excited, or uncontrolled

Keyword: friend's attic

He became **frenetic** after finding a rare baseball card in his **friend's attic**.

George was looking forward to retirement when he could put his **frenetic** life-style behind and just relax for a while.

[She] has been a harsh critic of children's programming—Mister Rogers excepted. Typically, she says, the **frenetic** pacing, adult irony and consumerist agenda is, at the very least, inappropriate.[169]

Anne Arundel County's new planning chief, whose **frenetic** work schedule has earned him the moniker [nickname] "Ironman," is rebuilding the county's planning office....[170]

write your own:

     http://SolidA.net

Fulsome

'ful-s&m

(Adjective) praise too positive to be considered sincere or genuine/ abundant; generous in amount
Keyword: full slum

Tremendously thankful for a place to sleep, the homeless man gave the **full slum** an extremely high **fulsome** rating.

The realtor's **fulsome** praise for the house was a little too unrealistic, and therefore we decided not to buy the home.

[President Franklin Delano Roosevelt's] typical campaign speech, the York Herald Tribune said, began with "a few words of **fulsome** praise for Alfred E. Smith."[171]

[He] was **fulsome** in his praise of Tim Byrne yesterday, saying his chief executive had done "an amazing job" and had his "total confidence."[172]

write your own: |

'f&r-tiv

(Adjective) done secretly so as not to be noticed by others

Keyword: fur live

The bear skin rug pretended to be dead during the day, but the **fur lived** at night by **furtively** eating leftovers.

Cindy suspected Peter had a secret crush on her after she caught him repeatedly casting **furtive** glances at her.

There was nothing **furtive** about the protest that took place in bright sunshine surrounding Cherry Cheek Shopping Center Friday. At least seven animal-rights groups ... joined forces, placards [posters] and passion in protesting swanky [fashionably elegant] shopping icon Neiman Marcus for selling furs.[173]

Most of his (characters) spend some of their time snatching **furtive** glimpses of people from behind their curtains ....[174]

write your own: |

Galvanize

'gal-v&-"nIz

(Verb) to shock someone or something into action
Keyword: gal's fan eyes

The **gal's fan eyes galvanized** the men back to work every time she winked at them.

The latest oil spill **galvanized** the local residents to support programs that promote alternative forms of energy.

Prior to the wars and political upheavals that would mark the next century, Krakatoa became the first story to **galvanize** world attention.[175]

How likely is it that other worlds harbor life? That's the question that **galvanizes** NASA and the wider public.[176]

write your own:

Garble

'gär-b&l

(Verb) to distort or alter (usually refers to a message)
Note: Garbled is a verb that functions like an adjective
Keyword: marble

Scientists tried to unravel the mystery of the ancient **marble** ruin, but the remaining fragments of the broken marble left the message **garbled** and undecipherable.

The 911 operator had a hard time deciphering the **garbled** message from the hysterical caller.

Because voice and video get crammed down the same thin phone line by the Beamer's built-in modem and compression software, our words at times came through **garbled** or not at all—like a bad cell-phone connection.[177]

Worse, a proposal for new merger [joining of companies] guidelines proved so **garbled** in its central definitions that it had to be withdrawn. A replacement is expected in a few weeks.[178]

write your own: |

Gregarious

gri-'gar-E-&s or gri-'ger-E-&s

(Adjective) enjoying the company of others;
outgoing or social
Keyword: hilarious

The **gregarious** young boy was always surrounded by
friends because he was so outgoing and **hilarious**.

Kelsey's **gregarious** personality made her a great candidate
for living in a sorority.

When hired, **gregarious** blackjack dealers and roulette spin-
ners give new meaning to having a game face: They wish gam-
blers luck, directing them to machines and tables that have
produced winners. When customers hit the jackpot, there are
high-fives and kudos.[179]

He doesn't smile a lot; he's not especially warm or **gregarious**; his dress is subdued and professional. Even his manner
of speaking is quiet, monotone, often stern and blunt.[180]

write your own: |

Gullible (Also gullable)

'g&-l&-b&l

(Adjective) easily deceived or tricked
Keyword: gull (as in sea gull)

The **gullible gull** ate seeds from the bird-catcher's hands.

They loved playing practical jokes on him because he was so **gullible**; he believed anything that he was told.

"I thought with enough help he could get his life going," says Harnish. "But he was a con artist, and I was **gullible**."[181]

He made room for mythical beasts and "monstrous humans" whose descriptions he **gullibly** accepted from seamen and other imaginative travelers.[182]

write your own: |

     http://SolidA.net

Hallow

'ha-lO

(Verb) to make holy/ much respected
Keyword: hollow

The **hollow** tree was **hallowed** by the local tribe as a sacred place of worship.

The flag is considered a **hallowed** and respected symbol for the United States of America.

There must be some legal basis for **hallowing** small pieces of ground—to give a guarantee that the ground a person chooses will not be sold and developed.[183]

Who here gave their lives that that nation might live. But in a larger sense we cannot dedicate, we cannot consecrate [to declare sacred], we cannot **hallow** this ground. The brave men, living and dead, who struggled here, have consecrated it far beyond our power to add or detract. - President Abraham Lincoln[184]

write your own:

Hedonist

'hE-d&n-ist

(Noun) a pleasure seeking person
Keyword: He done it!

Fred is a **hedonist** who spray paints buildings for the fun of it. He doubles his pleasure by pointing to someone else and yelling, "**He done it!**"

Concerned only for herself and her own pleasures, Marilyn is considered a **hedonist**.

If eating, drinking and shopping your way through Taipei has made you feel like a hopeless **hedonist**, the new Museum of World Religions... offers a cool, calm space for introspection [examining one's thoughts].[185]

When [Noah Webster] penned the first American dictionary, in 1825, he defined happiness as "the agreeable sensations which spring from the enjoyment of good." That says it all. It has "agreeable sensations," the notion that happiness is a feeling. The **hedonists** would get off on that.[186]

write your own:

Heretic

'her-&-"tik

(Noun) a person who holds an opinion or belief that is
against the principles of a particular religion

Keyword: hairy tick

He was considered a **heretic** because of his belief that no
living creature should be killed, not even the **hairy tick**
that suddenly appeared on his shoulder.

The **heretic** was removed from the ministry for his contro-
versial doctrinal beliefs.

The drought was so dire by August that Aurora council members considered a near-**heretical** move—limiting water taps.
That would mean limits on new housing and putting the brakes
on the city's cherished growth.[187]

The Puritan authorities considered Quakers **heretics** and ordered them banished from Massachusetts.[188]

write your own: _____

Hierarchy

'hI-"rär-kE or 'hI-&-"rär-kE

(Noun) a system where people are ranked at different levels according to their importance/ the upper level of people in authority
Keyword: high arches

The royal **hierarchy** lived in **high arches** that overlooked the city.

The caste system in India is a **hierarchical** system of several classes of people based on heredity, wealth, religion and customs.

In a study with monkeys, amphetamines [a type of drug] didn't seem to have an effect. Then the researchers looked at their social **hierarchy** and found that the drug increased the dominant behavior of the dominant animals and increased the submissive behavior of the submissive animals.[189]

Clothing has always been a clue to power relations, and one of the key ways to spot changes in social **hierarchies** is by looking at what people wore.[190]

write your own:

Iconoclast

I-'kä-n&-"klast

(Noun) a rebel; one who attacks the established beliefs, intuitions and traditions

Keyword: iron cast

An **iron cast** was created to honor the **iconoclast**, Robinhood, for taking from the rich and giving to the poor.

Williams, an **iconoclast** in the field of home-interior decoration, is renowned for making new homes look old and weathered.

Can a tiny company rooted in the Woodstock Generation make the transition from hippie to hipster? Birkenstock, best known for the ubiquitous [widespread] suede sandals worn by **iconoclasts** and counterculture types, is taking steps to find out.[191]

They're ore than smart investors. They're **iconoclasts** and trendsetters...[192]

write your own:

Impeach

im-'pEch

(Verb) to make a formal accusation (usually against a public official); to charge with a crime
Keyword: peach

The President was **impeached** for stealing the **peach**.

The House of Representatives has the authority to **impeach** and charge the President for committing a crime, while the Senate votes for conviction.

Browsing in a neighborhood antiques shop you spy a single ticket dated March 5, 1868, admitting the bearer to the U.S. Capitol where, in the Senate chamber, lawmakers debated whether to **impeach** President Andrew Johnson. [The effort failed.][193]

Disney claimed that the DreamWorks documents were necessary to **impeach** Katzenberg or his experts.[194]

write your own: |

Imperative

im-'per-&-tiv

(Adjective) essential; extremely urgent
Keyword: pear

The doctor informed his patient that it was **imperative** to eat **pears** to stay alive.

It is **imperative** to harvest the crops before the first freeze.

It's **imperative** that you focus on the fundamental few sales-people who'll afford you the lion's share of the results.[195]

Only in Washington would it be considered **imperative** to extend legislation precisely because it's been so ineffectual [unsuccessful].[196]

write your own: _____

Impetuous

im-'pech-w&s or im-'pe-ch-w&s

(Adjective) rash or impulsive
Keyword: a pet to us

The opossum became **a pet to us** after we made an **impetuous** decision at the last minute to rescue it from the local animal shelter.

He later regretted allowing the salesman to talk him into making an **impetuous** decision to buy a new car without selling his old one first.

[He was] described in court yesterday as "volatile and **impetuous**" and a "law unto herself...."[197]

Once awake, he made a number of snap judgments, some of them showing restraint and good sense, others demonstrating his sometimes **impetuous** nature.[198]

write your own: |

Impute

im-'pyüt

(Verb) to credit an action to a particular person or group
Keyword: chimp suit

WE BLAME YOU FOR THE MIX-UP!

The tailor was **imputed** in the **chimp suit** mix-up after the groom discovered that his tuxedo was mistakenly tailored for a chimp.

Environmentalists often **impute** global warming to corporations that are more interested in making money than taking care of their environment.

Readers often **impute** contrasting motives and conclusions to the same piece of journalism.[199]

At least it comes as no surprise to me; I prefer to **impute** as many everyday problems as possible to forces beyond my control....[200]

write your own:

Section 5 Crossword Puzzle

©Solid A, Inc.   http://SolidA.net

Across

1. having too much decoration; gaudy

5. irregular; occurring in spurts

7. a person who holds an opinion or belief that is against the principles of a particular religion

9. to shock someone or something into action

12. to make a formal accusation (usually against a public official); to charge with a crime

16. a rebel; one who attacks the established beliefs, intuitions, and traditions

17. rash or impulsive

18. a system where people are ranked at different levels, according to their importance/ the upper level of people in authority

Down

1. to disregard or disobey intentionally

2. easily deceived or tricked

3. nearly hopeless; deserted; sad and lonely due to isolation

4. done secretly so as not to be noticed by others

6. praise too positive to be considered sincere or genuine/ abundant

8. enjoying the company of others; outgoing

10. essential; extremely urgent

11. frantic, wildly excited, or uncontrolled

13. a pleasure seeking person

14. to distort or alter (usually refers to a message)

15. to credit an action to a particular person or group

18. to make holy/ much respected

Section 5 Multiple Choice Review

Select the word that best fits each sentence.

1. The travel agency created a slogan to attract _____: Take a vacation from your vacation and really have some fun.
    a. iconoclasts   b. heretics   c. hedonists   d. hierarchies

2. The furniture maker was well known for the extra hours he spent adding _____ details to each piece of furniture.
    a. imperative   b. imputed   c. florid   d. impetuous

3. After Suzy ran over a nail, it was _____ to change the flat tire before driving the car.
    a. impetuous   b. furtive   c. gullible   d. imperative

4. Sarah was _____ into finishing the spare bedroom when she heard of her mother-in-law's upcoming visit.
    a. imputed   b. flouted   c. galvanized   d. hallowed

5. After making her final decision she _____ bad taste to her friends who disagreed with her.
    a. impeached   b. imputed   c. flouted   d. galvanized

6. Martin Luther was once labeled a(n) _____, for his non-Catholic beliefs.
    a. hedonist   b. heretic   c. iconoclast   d. flout

7. Salesmen love to purchase lists of names and addresses of _____ people who will buy anything.
    a. gregarious   b. forlorn   c. hedonistic   d. gullible

8. Mark _____ his parents' rules by climbing out of his bedroom window to attend the party.
    a. flouted   b. hallowed   c. impeached   d. garbled

9. The rescue team's _____ attempts to retrieve the stranded hikers were unsuccessful due to the rapid changes in the weather conditions.
    a. fulsome   b. florid   c. furtive   d. fitful

10. The cable box unscrambles the _____ television images for each paid channel.
    a. garbled   b. frenetic   c. imperative   d. galvanized

11. The Unabomber, who sent mail bombs protesting people using technology, was hard to catch as he led a _____ existence in a small cabin in Montana far away from anyone else.
    a. furtive   b. heretical   c. gregarious   d. fulsome

12. Although exhausting, the _____ week leading up to the wedding reception was well worth it; all the preparation definitely paid off.
    a. frenetic   b. fitful   c. florid   d. forlorn

13. After seeing the awful movie, I told myself I would never again believe any incredibly positive, _____ reviews from that movie critic again.
    a. imperative   b. fulsome   c. galvanized   d. gregarious

14. My cat is very _____ and doesn't like to be by himself.
    a. furtive   b. gullible   c. gregarious   d. impetuous

15. Pope John Paul III is a(n) _____ figure for Catholics worldwide.
    a. iconoclastic   b. hierarchical   c. heretical   d. hallowed

16. The principal considered Frank a(n) _____, causing trouble and upheaval in the school. The students however looked up to Frank and admired his boldness.
    a. heretic   b. hedonist   c. iconoclast   d. flout

17. In a given class of students, a sort of _____ may form; the popular students may set themselves apart with an elitist status.
    a. hierarchy   b. heretic   c. iconoclast   d. impeachment

18. It is every President's nightmare to be _____ for wrongdoing.
    a. flouted   b. hallowed   c. impeached   d. galvanized

19. She had a very _____ personality when shopping and tended to make rash, and impulsive purchases.
    a. imputed   b. florid   c. garbled   d. impetuous

20. The _____ look on the lady's face told others she was recently widowed.
    a. hallowed   b. fitful   c. forlorn   d. frenetic

Section 5 Matching Review

Match the word on the left to the correct meaning on the right.

1. _____ Fitful
2. _____ Florid
3. _____ Flout
4. _____ Forlorn
5. _____ Frenetic
6. _____ Fulsome
7. _____ Furtive
8. _____ Galvanize
9. _____ Garble
10. _____ Gregarious
11. _____ Gullible
12. _____ Hallow
13. _____ Hedonist
14. _____ Heretic
15. _____ Hierarchy
16. _____ Iconoclast
17. _____ Impeach
18. _____ Imperative
19. _____ Impetuous
20. _____ Impute

A. to make a formal accusation (usually against a public official); to charge with a crime
B. to make holy/ much respected
C. rash or impulsive
D. to credit an action to a particular person or group
E. a person who holds an opinion or belief that is against a particular religion
F. having too much decoration; gaudy
G. to distort or alter (usually refers to a message)
H. frantic; wildly excited; uncontrolled
I. done secretly so as not to be noticed by others
J. essential; extremely urgent
K. praise too positive to be considered sincere or genuine/abundant
L. enjoying the company of others; outgoing
M. a system where people are ranked at different levels, according to their importance/ the upper level of people in authority
N. a pleasure seeking person
O. irregular; occurring in spurts
P. to shock someone or something into action
Q. a rebel; one who attacks the established beliefs, intuitions and traditions
R. easily deceived or tricked
S. to disregard or disobey intentionally
T. nearly hopeless; deserted; sad and lonely due to isolation

Section Six

Incongruous

in-'kä[ng]-gr&-w&s

(Adjective) different from what generally happens/
inappropriate or out of place
Keyword: in Congress

REP. ANDREWS
KANSAS

REP. ERNST
CALIFORNIA

REP. HAWTHORN
GEORGIA

The new representative looked very **incongruous** when he appeared **in Congress** without a shirt and with spiked hair.

Her unkempt room seemed **incongruous** in a house where everything was kept in perfect order.

Since a doctor who doesn't like sick people seems as **incongruous** as an investor who doesn't like risk, she began to question her chosen career.[201]

Most people have difficulty dealing with mixed messages of a verbal [spoken] nature. They are even more baffled by **incongruous** nonverbal ... messages.[202]

write your own: _____

©Solid A, Inc.   http://SolidA.net

Incursion

in-'k&r-zh&n

(Noun) a sudden attack or entrance; a hostile invasion
Keyword: in cursive

The threat of the **incursion** was written **in cursive** handwriting. It said, "Surrender, or we will attack suddenly. Sincerely, the enemy."

Heidi's big brother made an **incursion** into the living room during the sleepover and scared the girls.

Crowded with comforting groups of pottery animals, enamel boxes and porcelain figurines, the room gave the impression of belonging to a woman trying to protect herself from the **incursions** of the outside world. —Princess Diana's room[203]

We are learning to regulate [govern] to allow for the freedoms the Internet was intended to provide us, while at the same time guard against undeserved **incursions** on our privacy, like the ones spammers make....[204]

write your own: _____

Indigent

'in-di-j&nt

(Adjective) extremely poor or deficient
(Noun) a poor person
Keyword: in the tent

The **indigent** was so poor he lived **in the tent**.

Many criticize the welfare system saying it does not do enough to promote education and better job training for its **indigent** recipients.

In a poor Caracas [Venezuela] neighborhood, the conqueror was greeted not with roses but with bitter protest—a sign that the loathing [extreme disgust] he inspires in the middle and upper classes had dangerously percolated [penetrated] into even the **indigent** areas that had once invested such hopes in his revolution.[205]

He [was] one of the few psychiatrists anywhere willing to testify for **indigent** black defendants, and his research and testimony would play a crucial role in the landmark Brown v. Board of Education case that ended segregation [separation of races] in public schools.[206]

write your own:

Indomitable

in-'dä-m&-t&-b&l

(Adjective) incapable of being conquered
Keyword: in dominoes

In dominoes he was the **indomitable** world champion—
never losing a tournament.

The **indomitable** runner could not be kept from his work-
outs, not even if it was raining or snowing outside.

Seemingly **indomitable**, Microsoft boasts the best-selling
suite, the best-selling Windows word processor, a highly competitive spreadsheet, and all the leverage of its operating system architecture and programming tools.[207]

The [Oakland] A's of 1999, you see, were much like this
team—nearly **indomitable** at home, but profoundly iffy [un-
reliable] on the road.[208]

write your own:

Inimical

i-'ni-mi-k&l

(Adjective) hostile or unfriendly
Keyword: Indian nickel

The **inimical** coin collectors fought over the rare **Indian nickel.**

The landowners were **inimical** to anyone that tried to hunt on their land. They posted signs that read, "We shoot trespassers first and ask questions later."

The increased role of government has had many of the same adverse effects on higher education as on elementary and secondary education. It has fostered an atmosphere that both dedicated teachers and serious students often find **inimical** to learning.[209]

The mines were stable, not subject to cave-ins, and maintained a constant temperature and humidity that was not **inimical** to human comfort.[210]

write your own: |

Innocuous

i-'nä-ky&-w&s

(Adjective) harmless; not dangerous or hostile
Keyword: inoculate

While the child was **inoculated** for Polio, the doctor explained how the shot was **innocuous** and would not really hurt him.

The **innocuous** looking miniature poodle was not as docile as it looked. It had been known to attack and bite unfamiliar people.

Although most heart murmurs are relatively **innocuous**, some have serious causes. If a murmur is detected, the doctor has to decide based on its nature if a further evaluation is warranted.[211]

Most of President Bush's overseas trips are carefully scripted and largely risk-free occasions, notable for smiling photo ops [opportunities] and **innocuous** official statements, not for difficult diplomacy.[212]

write your own:

Insurgent

in-'s&r-j&nt

(Adjective) rebelling against established authority
(Noun) a rebel
Keyword: surgeon

The **surgeon** fixed the **insurgent** soldier's injuries despite the resistance he put up.

Unsatisfied with the results of the current political parties, an **insurgent** candidate was unanimously voted into office.

The war has come to a critical juncture. Prabhakaran, hidden somewhere in the jungles of the north, controls an **insurgent** army of 10,000, including a potent naval unit.[213]

They walked in silence for a moment past a display of captured **insurgent** flags that had been mounted under glass along the curved concrete wall.[214]

write your own:

Intransigence (also intransigeance)
in-'tran-s&-j&ns or in-'trant-s&-j&nts

(Noun) refusal to come to an agreement or compromise
Keyword: in a trance again

The hypnotist avoided any **intransigence** with his customers. If they would not agree to pay, he put them **in a trance again**.

Due to the angry workers' **intransigence**, their union refused to agree on a settlement.

Toan denied that he was financing the Jesuits' covert [secret] operation in Japan, but steadfastly refused to abjure [give up] his faith. Such **intransigence** infuriated the authorities....[215]

Their continued **intransigence** has done their members a serious disservice, and surely leaves the government with no choice but to impose a settlement....[216]

write your own: _____

Inundate

'i-n&n-"dAt

(Verb) to overwhelm; to flood with water
Keyword: on a date

On a date, the couple was **inundated** by a huge wave while walking on the beach.

After the tornado struck, the emergency line at the police station was **inundated** with calls for several hours from people requesting help.

Immediately after the crash, she was afraid family members would **inundate** her with as yet unanswerable questions about the cause.[217]

Ask the gambling industry to describe the economic benefits of casinos, and it will **inundate** you with a seemingly endless stream of statistics, reports and testimonials.[218]

write your own:

Invective

in-'vek-tiv

(Noun) a violent verbal attack or denunciation
(Adjective) relating to insult or abuse
Keyword: detective

After the verbal attack on the lady, she hired a **detective** to find the man that uttered the **invective**.

The well-known activist was notorious for his **invective** speeches that would shock his listeners.

George McGovern, the liberal Democrat who ran against President Richard Nixon in 1972 and lost every state except Massachusetts and the District of Columbia, is a quiet man not given to **invectives** or I-told-you-sos.[219]

[Famous Psychologist] Sigmund Freud famously argued that satire [a form of ridicule] and **invective** constituted [made up] a form of not-very-concealed [not well hidden] aggression.[220]

write your own: |

Jargon

'jär-g&n or 'jär-"gän

(Noun) specialized language; technical terminology
Keyword: jar gone

The **jargon** of the Egyptian priests was encrypted on two jars. With one **jar gone**, their language remains a mystery.

The **jargon** computer programmers use to communicate is undecipherable to most people.

Finally, artists should not be deterred by unfamiliar technology. After wading through the **jargon**, artists will find that, as in art, much can be learned through experimentation.[221]

Immediately following its 1994 debut [introduction], the NBC drama ... became a breakthrough hit with its doctors spouting medical **jargon** and juggling needles, scalpels and defibrillators.[222]

write your own: |

Lackluster

'lak-"l&s-t&r

(Adjective) dull, lacking brightness, or mediocre
Keyword: lacked mustard

The hotdog stand reportedly had such **lackluster** service, they even **lacked mustard**.

The store-owner worried about **lackluster** sales during the summer months since construction on the freeway routed many of his customers far away from the store.

The Revolution needed a quality home win after two straight **lackluster** performances at Gillette Stadium....[223]

I rode once more, at a dude ranch, but that experience has never seemed to count. The horse was so old, so **lackluster**, so much the workhorse (and thus obviously, to everyone's amusement, so perfect for me) that I might as well have been taking a cab.[224]

write your own: |

Laconic

l&-'kä-nik

(Adjective) using few words; concise
Keyword: lack of

Because the driver was **laconic**, the passenger complained about the **lack of** communication during the long trip.

He opened his mouth just enough to let out a few **laconic** remarks.

He has never joined any group, party, or discussion in any way other than silently. Stealth is in his nature. He is **laconic** and cautious and light on his feet.[225]

Volz is a curious combination of reticence [keeping to one's self] and daring, unafraid to leap brashly [boldly or audaciously] off catwalks [platforms] 55 feet high in Indiana's field house but **laconic** even with his good friends.[226]

write your own:

©Solid A, Inc.   http://SolidA.net

Lampoon

lam-'pün

(Noun) a written attack against someone or something
(Verb) to attack someone or something in writing or speech
Keyword: lamp spoon

Larry wrote a harsh **lampoon** against the new **lamp spoon** invention, after people received severe electric shocks when they turned it on.

Mark Twain was fond of criticizing and creating **lampoons** of President Theodore Roosevelt.

He was living a life of retirement near Geneva, safe from the attacks of Church and State in France, whose enmity [hostility] he had provoked by satire, **lampoon**, and ridicule directed against their authoritarian rule.[227]

On October 2, 1953, the witty [intelligent] Borge opened at his theatre in a one-man show called "Comedy in Music." Mr. Borge played the piano and indulged in ... **lampoons** that kept audiences in stitches for 849 performances.[228]

write your own:

'lA-t$^{\&}$nt

(Adjective) present but inactive;
having unforeseen potential
Keyword: late ant

The **late ant's latent** talent was never discovered because he never arrived to his music lessons on time.

Unaware that she was harboring a grudge towards her friend, her **latent** anger exploded after her friend lied to her.

On one ride a **latent** terror of heights suddenly overwhelmed an otherwise peaceful man named Wherritt. He was fine until the car began to move.[229]

Another possible explanation is that stress compromises immune function in women, activating **latent** infections and increasing the likelihood of preterm delivery.[230]

write your own: |

Laudable

'lo-d&-b&l

(Adjective) praiseworthy or admirable
Keyword: loud Able

Loud Able was given a standing ovation for his **laudable** and praiseworthy speech.

He was recognized and thanked for his **laudable** efforts in developing a new park that will greatly benefit the kids in the community.

Educators, long disturbed by schoolchildren's lagging scores in math and reading, are realizing there is a different and more alarming deficiency: emotional illiteracy. And while **laudable** efforts are being made to raise academic standards, this new and troubling deficiency is not being addressed in the standard school curriculum.[231]

What you're doing [building schools] for the students of Baltistan is most **laudable**.[232]

write your own: _____

Lethargy

'le-th&r-jE

(Noun) drowsiness; state of sluggishness and inactivity

Keyword: leather

CHEMICAL
LEATHER TREATMENT

The chemicals used to treat **leather** at his job left him in a state of **lethargy**.

His **lethargy** was brought on by pure exhaustion; he had not slept for four consecutive nights since the new baby was brought home.

What's more, on one visit to altitude you may be fine, but on the next you could be struck down with the headaches, nausea, disorientation and **lethargy** that are the hallmarks of AMS [Acute Mountain Sickness].[233]

Enlistment centers were overwhelmed by the flood of eager enlistees. The entire nation, in fact, seemed overnight to have snapped out of its Depression-era **lethargy**. Everyone scrambled to be of help.[234]

write your own: |

Listless

'list-l&s

(Adjective) without energy, enthusiasm, or interest
Keyword: list

The children felt **listless** about their mother's grocery **list** until she added ice cream.

Despite all of the treatments for her illness, the girl remained **listless** on her bed, refusing to sit up or eat.

Although such new acts as Hootie and The Blowfish, Alanis Morissette and Green Day have sold millions of albums, they have not been able to lift a **listless** market.[235]

The mental faculties are often much impaired ... difficult attention is very often present. The child is **listless** and has difficulty in applying himself continuously to his play, studies, or other tasks, of which he soon tires.[236]

write your own: |

m&-'le-v&-l&nt

(Adjective) ill-willed/ causing evil or harm to others
Keyword: [shopping] mall devil

The **malevolent** "**Mall Devil**" caused bad things to happen to the shoppers.

His reputation as a **malevolent** person made me leery of being his friend.

Plunging through 2 feet of water to her office stairs, she saw all around her evidence of nature's **malevolent** power.[237]

The pit's **malevolent** red eye—obscured [hidden] by gases and a balcony ledge of new volcanic rock—sits just a few hundred feet below.[238]

write your own:

Melancholy

'me-l&n-"kä-lE

(Noun) sadness or depression
(Adjective) sad or gloomy
Keyword: melon collie

Because our dog devoured all of the melons in the garden when he felt sad and **melancholy**, we nicknamed him "**Melon Collie**."

After a few months, his **melancholy** demeanor was beginning to affect the attitudes of his close friends, making them feel blue.

A queenless colony [of bees] is a pitiful and **melancholy** community; there may be a mournful wail or lament from within... Without intervention, the colony will die. [239]

He had no energy, and the bigger he got, the less he played. Sluggishness eventually weighted him to the lawn chair and tending the grill, where he cooked burgers and ribs, and drank longneck beers with a twist of **melancholy**.[240]

write your own: |

Section 6 Crossword Puzzle

©Solid A, Inc. http://SolidA.net

Across

1. a written attack against someone or something

3. sadness, depression, or gloomy

6. extremely poor; deficient/ a poor person

9. praiseworthy or admirable

11. a violent verbal attack; denunciation

16. harmless; not dangerous or hostile

17. refusal to come to an agreement or compromise

18. without energy, enthusiasm, or interest

Down

1. drowsiness; state of sluggishness and inactivity

2. present but inactive; having unforeseen potential

4. to overwhelm; to flood with water

5. hostile or unfriendly

7. specialized language; technical terminology

8. a sudden attack or entrance; a hostile invasion

10. dull, lacking brightness, or mediocre

12. different from what generally happens/ inappropriate or out of place

13. incapable of being conquered

14. using few words; concise

15. ill-willed/ causing evil or harm to others

17. rebelling against established authority; a rebel

Section 6 Multiple Choice Review

Select the word that best fits each sentence.

1. Many people possess a _____ talent for art yet never discover it.
   a. latent   b. lackluster   c. indigent   d. indomitable

2. Thomas loved to use the medical _____ from his textbooks to try to impress his classmates and professor.
   a. lampoons   b. invectives   c. jargon   d. incursions

3. He felt like a knife had penetrated his heart when he read the harmful _____ written about him.
   a. jargon   b. intransigence   c. incursion   d. lampoon

4. The student's oral report seemed rather _____, and fell far short of the required time.
   a. listless   b. melancholy   c. laconic   d. malevolent

5. Cathy likes to give money to every _____ beggar she sees.
   a. laudable   b. indigent   c. incongruous   d. inimical

6. The company's effort to recycle all of their byproducts is _____ and has earned them a lot of recognition in the community.
   a. insurgent   b. laudable   c. malevolent   d. latent

7. The kids look up to their dad as a(n) _____ fire fighter who is the strongest, bravest man in the world.
   a. indomitable   b. listless   c. lethargic   d. indigent

8. The new renters were _____ and prone to fighting other people in their apartment complex.
   a. indomitable   b. inimical   c. innocuous   d. melancholy

9. Although she had no _____ intentions, she caused a great deal of harm by having the local animal shelter shut down.
   a. malevolent   b. laconic   c. lackluster   d. listless

10. The Venus flytrap seems completely _____ to unsuspecting flies, until they get too close.
    a. incongruous   b. inimical   c. innocuous   d. lackluster

11. The new arts center looked strangely _____ in the impoverished section of town.
   a. malevolent   b. laconic   c. innocuous   d. incongruous

12. The _____ movement led to a coup that overthrew the former government.
   a. latent   b. innocuous   c. invective   d. insurgent

13. The car salesman tried very hard to reverse the couple's decision about which car they were going to buy, but their _____ was immovable.
   a. intransigence   b. lethargy   c. incursion   d. invective

14. The _____ written in the editorial column denounced the politician for pocketing government money, and called the senator a thief.
   a. jargon   b. incursion   c. invective   d. insurgent

15. Sue's _____ effort on the basketball team earned her a spot on the bench.
   a. lackluster   b. laconic   c. latent   d. laudable

16. The other workers at Dana's job complained about her constant _____, stating that they frequently caught her sleeping.
   a. incursions   b. intransigence   c. lethargy   d. invectives

17. The average American sits _____ in front of the television for over four hours a day.
   a. latent   b. malevolent   c. irascible   d. listless

18. A moat was built around the castle to help ward off any further enemy _____.
   a. intransigence   b. jargons   c. incursions   d. lampoons

19. Her _____ behavior after giving birth was diagnosed as post partum depression.
   a. indigent   b. melancholy   c. inimical   d. insurgent

20. In the springtime, the real estate agency finds itself _____ with thousands of people looking for new homes.
   a. incongruous   b. inundated   c. inimical   d. laconic

Section 6 Matching Review

Match the word on the left to the correct meaning on the right.

1. ____ Incongruous
2. ____ Incursion
3. ____ Indigent
4. ____ Indomitable
5. ____ Inimical
6. ____ Innocuous
7. ____ Insurgent
8. ____ Intransigence
9. ____ Inundate
10. ____ Invective
11. ____ Jargon
12. ____ Lackluster
13. ____ Laconic
14. ____ Lampoon
15. ____ Latent
16. ____ Laudable
17. ____ Lethargy
18. ____ Listless
19. ____ Malevolent
20. ____ Melancholy

A. different from what generally happens/ inappropriate or out of place
B. extremely poor; deficient/ a poor person
C. specialized language; technical terminology
D. using few words; concise
E. a written attack against someone or something
F. harmless; not dangerous or hostile
G. refusal to come to an agreement or compromise
H. ill-willed/ causing evil or harm to others
I. a sudden attack or entrance; a hostile invasion
J. praiseworthy or admirable
K. a violent verbal attack; denunciation
L. drowsiness; state of sluggishness and inactivity
M. incapable of being conquered
N. present but inactive; having unforeseen potential
O. without energy, enthusiasm, or interest
P. to overwhelm; to flood with water
Q. sadness; depression; gloomy
R. hostile or unfriendly
S. rebelling against established authority; a rebel
T. dull, lacking brightness, or mediocre

Section Seven

Mnemonic

ni-'mä-nik

(Adjective) assisting the memory
Keyword: new mom

The **new mom** used **mnemonic** devices to remember the names of her newborn octuplets.

Chad discovered that using **mnemonic** devices to study for the test was the best way to remember the material.

Another enduring **mnemonic** is how to tell the difference between stalactites and stalagmites [rock formations in caves]: stalactites hang on tight to make sure they don't fall off; stalagmites try with all their might to grow upwards.[241]

To ignite your memory power, try the following **mnemonic** techniques. Trigger words. Instead of trying to remember an entire story or speech word-for-word, use a few word cues.[242]

write your own:

Munificence

myu-'ni-f&-s&nts or myu-'ni-f&-s&ns

(Noun) the quality of being extremely generous
Keyword: new fifty cents

When the **new fifty cent** pieces were first introduced, the **munificent** coin collector gave away thousands out of generosity.

The town rapturously thanked Paul Newman for his **munificence**. Due to his generous donations, the town was able to rebuild after being destroyed by a tornado.

[I will] appease him with all **munificence**. Here before everyone I may enumerate the gifts I'll give. Seven new tripods and ten bars of gold, then twenty shining caldrons, and twelve horses....[243]

Do we want to contemplate his **munificence**? We see it in the abundance with which he fills the earth.[244]

write your own: |

Nascent

'na-s&nt or 'nA-s&nt

(Adjective) starting to develop,
recently started, or brand new
Keyword: NASA sent

NASA sent a **nascent** research module with the latest technological innovations to the international space station.

The **nascent** tree was well known for how much fruit it produced just months after being planted.

He shifted the attaché case to his left hand and was aware of the book, like a tumor, he thought, **nascent** at the moment, newly discovered, awaiting diagnosis.[245]

There is a **nascent** effort to translate emotional skills into software that will "humanize" computers.[246]

write your own:

Nefarious

ni-'far-E-&s or ni-'fer-E-&s

(Adjective) evil or wicked
Keyword: not far

When the **nefarious** queen, scheming to kill Snow White, asked the enchanted mirror where she was, the mirror replied, "**Not far.**"

It was recently uncovered that the company had been participating in **nefarious** activities and that the owner was the head of the mafia.

These lawmakers fear information readily available in government records can be used for **nefarious** reasons, including terrorist attacks, identity theft, fraud, and invasion of privacy.[247]

Tropico 2 lets you don [put on] an eye patch and wooden leg to control a Caribbean island full of **nefarious** buccaneers [pirates].[248]

write your own: _____

Noisome

'noi-s&m

(Adjective) offensive or harmful
(especially to the senses)
Note: This word is not related to noise
Keyword: noise

The continuous loud **noise** that came from the garage was actually **noisome** "music" played by the local teenage band.

The **noisome** garbage piled up in front of the apartments as the city sanitation workers continued their strike.

Restaurants are too expensive and noisy, pubs too smoke-filled and **noisome**, television too unspeakable....[249]

In the minds of most baseball fans, the **noisome** strike that has idled [stalled or stopped] the game has also raised troubling questions—such as, whose side to take in a war of words among millionaires.[250]

write your own: |

©Solid A, Inc.   http://SolidA.net

Nomenclature

'nO-m&n-"klA-ch&r

(Noun) a set of names or terms
the act of designating or choosing a name
Keyword: no men

No men were on the committee to set up the **nomenclature** for the newly discovered insects. They were, therefore, all named after women.

Eskimo **nomenclature** uses dozens of words to describe the different types of snow.

Check out job descriptions and start learning the **nomenclature**.[251]

Although the two disciplines overlap considerably, taxonomy is more concerned with **nomenclature** (naming) and with constructing hierarchial [grouping] systems, and systematics with uncovering evolutionary relationships.[252]

write your own: |

Obfuscate

'äb-f&-"skAt or äb-'f&s-"kAt

(Verb) to make something more difficult
to understand; to obscure
Keyword: office skate

The introduction of "**office skates**" into the work area resulted in a terrific mess that mixed up and **obfuscated** the
reports and files.

The technical vocabulary in the manual **obfuscated** the in-
structions, resulting in an extra hour of assembly.

The book's main weakness is that the arguments are not always cogently [convincingly] expressed and sometimes **obfuscate** rather than clarify the issues—a common weakness
of works written by academics for academics.[253]

The highest profile male in the women's game, didn't flinch,
dodge or **obfuscate** when the question was put to him recently: "Are male coaches in women's basketball in danger
of going the way of the dinosaur?"[254]

write your own:

Obsequious

&b-'sE-kwE-&s or äb-'sE-kwE-&s

(Adjective) too willing to serve or obey;
servile; overly submissive
Keyword: sequins

CLEAN FASTER, YOU!

The mean step-mother dressed in **sequins**, wished her step-daughter was more **obsequious**. She should not only want to do all the servile work in the house, but she should be happy doing it.

A marriage counselor recommended that if Robert wanted to save his marriage, he should cultivate a more **obsequious** attitude toward his wife and let her take charge sometimes.

"That book doesn't have fifty words in it that were changed by the editor!" exclaimed one author. "They were so respectful of my judgment, they were **obsequious**," said another.[255]

He began by writing an **obsequious** letter to Hitler, hailing him as "the great designer of German existence."[256]

write your own:

Omnipotent

äm-'ni-p&-t&nt

(Adjective) having unlimited power
Keyword: mom's hippo tent

After emerging from **mom's hippo tent**, my mom became the **omnipotent** SUPER HIPPO hero, having unlimited power.

As the first doctor in the camp, he was treated like an **omnipotent** being, able to seemingly cure the villager's diseases.

He might be a Mighty Duck, but he's not **omnipotent**. It might seem as if he is everywhere when he makes save after save, but he is not omnipresent [present everywhere].[257]

Both shots rocketed off a giant pine that had stood 35 years. The next day, the tree fell during a rainstorm. Arnie's devout followers are convinced their **omnipotent** idol [pro golfer], not Mother Nature, toppled the majestic tree.[258]

write your own:

©Solid A, Inc. http://SolidA.net

Ossify

'ä-s&-"fI

(Verb) to become rigid or fixed in place; to become bone; to become set in one's ways
Keyword: office fly

After months of being stuck on the glue strip, the **office fly ossified** and became rock hard.

The professor's teaching methods had become so outdated and **ossified** that he was no longer able to relate to his students.

They blame local authority employers for allowing terms and conditions to **ossify** over 25 years, during which the Fire Brigades Union refused to discuss changes to outdated working practices.[259]

The dried-up creek bed didn't just have one color, it had dozens, all combinations of the basic four colors—dark red hematite, lemon yellow, white pipeclay and black manganese that looked like chewing gum spat out by dinosaurs and left to **ossify**. The colored stones and pebbles were strewn in every direction.[260]

write your own:

Ostentatious

"äs-t&n-'tA-sh&s

(Adjective) showy; displaying wealth
Keyword: Austin [Texas]

The **ostentatious** capital building in **Austin**, Texas is a tourist attraction, with large expensive paintings and inlaid marble interior.

Our **ostentatious** neighbors held huge parties to show off their wealth.

He arrived [at Yahoo] expecting to see an incredible **ostentatious** display of wealth. At the time, a full three-quarters of the employees were millionaires. But they were still working in cubicles. Even the founders![261]

In the middle of the capital squats an **ostentatious** monument that marks the tomb of the unknown soldier.[262]

write your own: |

©Solid A, Inc.   http://SolidA.net

Palliate

'pa-lE-"At

(Verb) to make something appear less serious than it is
relieve without curing
Keyword: pal ate

Our **pal ate** a gallon of ice cream to **palliate** the pain he felt after being turned down for a date.

Attempting to **palliate** her boy's fears after he fell down, the mother covered up the scrape on his leg so he couldn't see the blood.

They are too embarrassed to confess their sins [openly], lest their confessors should think less of them, so they **palliate** them and make them appear less evil, and thus it is to excuse themselves rather than to accuse themselves that they go to confession.[263]

Attired in an old army coat worn in the Mexican War and a broken-visored V.M.I. cadet Captain Jackson constantly sucked lemons to **palliate** his dyspepsia [indigestion] and refused to season his food with pepper because (he said) it made his left leg ache.[264]

write your own: _____

Panegyric

"pa-n&-'jir-ik or "pa-n&-'jI-rik

(Noun) a formal, elaborate speech of praise
Keyword: pen of lyrics

The **pen of lyrics** sings **panegyric** praises and affirmations to increase your self-esteem.

The **panegyric** in the paper praised the new editor for his accomplishments and qualifications.

The Secret History—so named by Chinese archivists [keepers of historical documents—seems to be more than a **panegyric** written to enhance [Genghis Khan's] reputation.[265]

There was no sarcasm intended, it being part of a longer **panegyric**.[266]

write your own: |

Parsimony

'pär-s&-"mO-nE

(Noun) being stingy or excessively
careful with one's money
Keyword: purse of money

The children accused the mother of **parsimony**: she had a
purse of money but refused to buy them any toys.

For reasons of **parsimony**, Mary decided to buy an older
model car that was more affordable.

A major stumbling block has been money. Donor fatigue and
parsimony have led to major shortfalls in funds for control
programs.[267]

Instead of practical wisdom, such as "A penny saved is a penny
earned," we are given **parsimonious** exhortations [advice]
to transform dryer lint into Halloween costumes.[268]

write your own:

Paucity

'po-s&-tE

(Noun) scarcity or lack of number
Keyword: paw city (as in the paw of an animal)

In **Paw City** there is a **paucity** of people, but many animals.

Cowboys had to dance by themselves because of the **paucity** of women in the old west.

The most alarming aspect of New York's plan is that the Rangers have been left with a **paucity** of quality players between the ages of 24 and 29—the young veterans who form the core of many NHL teams on the rise.[269]

Many possible causes of the second Comet crash were put forward, but no conclusion could be reached with the **paucity** of evidence available.[270]

write your own: |

©Solid A, Inc.   http://SolidA.net

Peregrinate

'per-&-gr&-"nAt

(Verb) to wander or travel from place to place
Keyword: pair of grenades

Stuck with a **pair of grenades**, the soldier **peregrinated** for miles, searching for a safe spot to detonate them.

The group **peregrinated** several kilometers down the main street to display their signs and demonstrate their dedication to the cause.

I asked if she didn't think it insufferable that a 10-year-old should be pressed to provide official documentation to travel from one city to another. She looked at me sharply: "Doesn't your son have a passport?"
[She replied] "To **peregrinate** within our native homeland?"[271]

Join the thousands of music lovers from all over the world who **peregrinate** to the Delta Blues Museum, located in an 1812 train depot at the edge of town.[272]

write your own:

Perfunctory

p&r-'f&[ng]k-t&-rE

(Adjective) performed without care or
interest/ done automatically
Keyword: purr factory

Adding the purr to the toy kittens at the **purr factory** was a **perfunctory** job that the workers could do with their eyes closed.

She read the book in such a **perfunctory** manner that the book club members thought she wasn't interested in it.

But before leaving us, the President [Roosevelt] looked for the mechanic, shook his hand, called him by name and thanked him for coming to Washington. And there was nothing **perfunctory** about his thanks. He meant what he said. I could feel that.[273]

An annual Division of Insurance competition hearing that had been so **perfunctory** in the past that the commissioner once skipped it, yesterday filled a Boston conference room to over-flowing....[274]

write your own: |

Pernicious

p&r-'ni-sh&s

(Adjective) harmful or destructive; deadly
Keyword: perm fishes (as in curling the "hair" on a fish)

Many people thought that Jane's idea to **perm fishes** was a cruel and **pernicious** thing to do.

The **pernicious** termites ate into the wooden foundation of the house, costing thousands of dollars in damage.

Radioactivity wasn't banned in consumer products until 1938. By this time it was much too late for Madame Curie, who died of leukemia in 1934. Radiation, in fact, is so **pernicious** and long lasting that even now her papers from the 1890s—even her cookbooks—are too dangerous to handle.[275]

Tragically, America's forests ... are being decimated at an alarming rate by large-scale catastrophic wildfire and massive outbreaks of disease and insect infestation. Each year, millions of acres of once-pristine forestland are ravaged by these **pernicious** wildland scourges .[276]

write your own: |

'pI-&-tE

(Noun) devotion or reverence
Keyword: pie and tea

Before his favorite snack of **pie and tea**, the priest showed **piety** towards God by asking grace.

As a sign of Islamic **piety**, Fatima wears a veil over her hair when she ventures outside.

[His] **piety** is admirable. In these troubled times it's good to see a boy so keen on God.[277]

Fell's translation leaves no doubt that the carver of the inscriptions was a Christian. Even a novice can recognize one piece of evidence, the Chi-Rho—written "XP"—an ancient symbol of Christian **piety**.[278]

write your own:

'pEk

(Noun) resentment at being slighted; a feeling of hurt pride
(Verb) to provoke intrigue or interest
Keyword: peak

Tom was **piqued** at Jim who erroneously took all the credit
in the news for reaching the **peak** of the mountain first.

The biggest thing damaged in the motorcycle accident was
David's pride, but his **pique** quickly disappeared when he
realized how lucky he was to be uninjured.

The story goes that the mural was made hurriedly, in a fit of
pique after an argument....[279]

On the other hand, children who are truly loved, although in
moments of **pique** they may consciously feel or proclaim that
they are being neglected, unconsciously know themselves to
be valued.[280]

write your own:

Section 7 Crossword Puzzle

©Solid A, Inc.   http://SolidA.net

Across

2. showy; displaying wealth

4. offensive or harmful (especially to the senses)

6. resentment at being slighted; a feeling of hurt pride/ to provoke, intrigue, or interest

8. a set of names or terms; the act of designating or choosing a name

10. starting to develop, recently started, or brand new

11. the quality of being extremely generous

12. devotion or reverence

13. having unlimited power

15. to make something more difficult to understand; to obscure

17. evil or wicked

18. scarcity; lack of number

Down

1. harmful or destructive

3. too willing to serve or obey; servile; overly submissive

5. assisting the memory

6. to make something appear less serious than it is/ relieve without curing

7. to wander or travel from place to place

9. to become rigid or fixed in place/ to become bone

12. performed without care or interest/ done automatically

14. being stingy or excessively careful with one's money

16. a formal, elaborate speech of praise

Section 7 Multiple Choice Review

Select the word that best fits each sentence.

1. Because of his _____ reputation in the community, no one was surprised when he was arrested for the local homicide.
   a. ostentatious   b. parsimonious   c. obsequious   d. nefarious

2. The infomercial bragged about the _____ product not yet available at stores.
   a. obsequious   b. omnipotent   c. nascent   d. pernicious

3. Tanner was _____ at the derisive criticism from the class, and consequently he harbored a grudge towards many of his classmates.
   a. morose   b. piqued   c. obfuscated   d. palliated

4. Instead of healing her injury, the iodine the nurse used had a(n) _____ effect and made the cut worse.
   a. morose   b. obsequious   c. omnipotent   d. pernicious

5. The biologists used scientific _____ to name and classify the different organisms.
   a. nomenclature   b. mnemonics   c. pique   d. panegyrics

6. Jill demonstrates _____ towards God by praying before every meal.
   a. pique   b. parsimony   c. paucity   d. piety

7. The book was criticized for _____ the issue it was advertised to clarify.
   a. palliating   b. obfuscating   c. ossifying   d. peregrinating

8. For the sunny afternoon, we decided to _____ down to the park to have a picnic.
   a. ossify   b. obfuscate   c. peregrinate   d. palliate

9. Because she was so eager to help out, her _____ work ethic helped her earn a promotion at her job much faster than most of her co-workers.
   a. perfunctory   b. nascent   c. obsequious   d. pernicious

10. The employees of the large company could tell that the presi dent of the company made far more money than they did as a result of his _____ lifestyle.
    a. parsimonious   b. ostentatious   c. omnipotent   d. nefarious

11. The young boy was fascinated with his father's strength, and con-sidered him _____.
    a. munificent   b. ostentatious   c. perfunctory   d. omnipotent

12. After the cast was placed on his leg, the bone took several months to _____.
    a. ossify   b. obfuscate   c. peregrinate   d. palliate

13. Maria's doctor prescribed aspirin to _____ the pain in her foot.
    a. ossify   b. peregrinate   c. palliate   d. obfuscate

14. The best man's _____ at the wedding reception was sentimen-tal and told of some of his favorite times with the groom.
    a. munificence   b. paucity   c. piety   d. panegyric

15. For reasons of _____, the college students chose not to turn on their air conditioners on hot days, using fans instead.
    a. parsimony   b. paucity   c. nomenclature   d. piety

16. Upon discovering the source of the _____ stench, Nathan was horrified to find a dead skunk underneath the back porch.
    a. nascent   b. morose   c. parsimonious   d. noisome

17. In many third world countries there is a _____ of school sup-plies. Paper and pencils are luxury items that cannot be afforded.
    a. pique   b. paucity   c. perfunctory   d. parsimony

18. In order for her students to learn the fifty states more quickly, the teacher developed _____ sayings for them to rehearse.
    a. mnemonic   b. pernicious   c. panegyric   d. nefarious

19. Mike's weekly chores became so _____ he could perform them quickly with his eyes closed.
    a. mnemonic   b. morose   c. perfunctory   d. ostentatious

20. A grand banquet was given to thank the donors for their _____.
    a. piety   b. munificence   c. panegyrics   d. parsimony

Section 7 Matching Review

Match the word on the left to the correct meaning on the right.

1. _____ Mnemonic
2. _____ Munificence
3. _____ Nascent
4. _____ Nefarious
5. _____ Noisome
6. _____ Nomenclature
7. _____ Obfuscate
8. _____ Obsequious
9. _____ Omnipotent
10. _____ Ossify
11. _____ Ostentatious
12. _____ Palliate
13. _____ Panegyric
14. _____ Parsimony
15. _____ Paucity
16. _____ Peregrinate
17. _____ Perfunctory
18. _____ Pernicious
19. _____ Piety
20. _____ Pique

A. evil or wicked
B. the quality of being extremely generous
C. too willing to serve or obey; servile; overly submissive
D. offensive; harmful (especially to the senses)
E. having unlimited power
F. being stingy or excessively careful with one's money
G. assisting the memory
H. to wander or travel from place to place
I. a formal, elaborate speech of praise
J. showy; displaying wealth
K. to make something more difficult to understand; to obscure
L. starting to develop, recently started, or brand new
M. harmful or destructive
N. devotion or reverence
O. performed without care or interest/ done automatically
P. to make something appear less serious than it is/ relieve without curing
Q. to become rigid or fixed in place/ to become bone
R. scarcity; lack of number
S. resentment at being slighted; a feeling of hurt pride/ to provoke, intrigue or interest
T. a set of names or terms; the act of choosing a name

Section Eight

Plausible

'plo-z&-b&l

(Adjective) likely to be true; believable
Keyword: applause

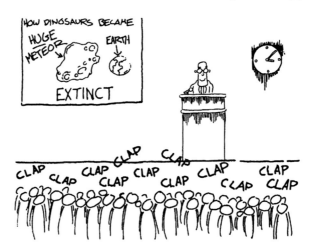

The scientific theory seemed so **plausible** that the audience's **applause** lasted for ten minutes.

The boy's excuse for coming home late seemed **plausible** until the owner of the video arcade called to say he left his backpack behind.

The former physicist had created a **plausible** model for the structure of DNA that morning. If they were right, biologists would finally understand how parents pass characteristics on to their children—not only hair and eye color but every aspect of how the human body is built and how it operates.[281]

There exists a multitude of unscientific and ethically dubious [questionable] interventions that are readily available (for a price). All can cite anecdotal evidence [based on observations], testimonials that make their methods sound as **plausible** as they are infallible [foolproof].[282]

write your own:

©Solid A, Inc.   http://SolidA.net

'plI-&nt

(Adjective) yielding; easily manipulated or changed
Keyword: pliers

Using **pliers** the artist was able to bend the **pliant** wires into an artistic masterpiece.

As he added more water, the clay became more **pliant** and easier to mold.

Though Peru's constitution limits presidents to two terms, the country's **pliant** courts and Congress have allowed him to stand for a third.[283]

Warren Buffett ... said **pliant** directors who failed to ask tough questions or fire executives are partly to blame for the recent corporate catastrophes.[284]

write your own: |

Polemic

(Noun) an attack or defense regarding a set of principles, ideals, or opinions; argument; debate; controversy

Keyword: pole limit

The fisherman engaged in a **polemic** with the park warden, arguing that he was unhappy with the new **pole limit** of one fishing pole per family.

The televised **polemic** uncovered many scandals that the governor's administration had desperately been trying to conceal.

History is the **polemics** of the victor. -William F. Buckley, Jr.[285]

Shortly before his death he "lashed out at his critics in a **polemic** ... that charged them with perpetuating [carrying on] myths...."[286]

write your own: |

Pompous

'päm-p&s

(Adjective) self-important or arrogant
Keyword: pom-poms

The **pom-poms** made the cheerleader feel **pompous** and more important than others.

Miss America was accused of being **pompous** and arrogant when she refused a TV interview because the station had too few viewers.

Unlike his photos—where he looks like a stern, **pompous** politician—he was a warm, generous man.[287]

Drawing attention to himself as a loud, **pompous**, self-important official would make an impression, he reasoned, and he wanted the guard to remember him.[288]

write your own: |

Precipitous

pri-'si-p&-t&s

(Adjective) very steep

Keyword: pressed lips

Several pairs of **pressed lips** smashed against the front window of the bus as it descended the **precipitous** mountain road.

Due to high interest rates and job layoffs, there was a **precipitous** fall in the sale of houses.

With the deep cuts [in jobs] came a **precipitous** drop in the airline's once-enviable customer service ratings. Complaints about Delta suddenly skyrocketed—everything from dirty planes and late departures to missing baggage.[289]

Entering last night's contest against Indiana, a 102-72 Celtics' loss, there had been a **precipitous** dip in Boston's 3-point shooting percentage over the last two games.[290]

write **own:**
your

                    http://SolidA.net

Predilection

"pre-d&l-'ek-sh&n or "prE-d&l-'ek-sh&n

(Noun) a preconceived liking; a preference
for something
Keyword: election

California voters seem to have a **predilection** for movie star
candidates up for **election**-- voting several into office.

Danielle took a **predilection** to swimming when she was a
child, and now she works every summer as a lifeguard.

The movie isn't as clever by half as Herrington's previous "A
Murder of Crows," which pitted lawyer Cuba Gooding Jr.
against a villain with a penchant [strong liking] for disguise
and a **predilection** for literature.[291]

He was also a direct male-line descendant of Genghis Khan, though
intervening generations and racial mixing had so juggled his genes that
he had no discernible Mongoloid characteristics, and the only vestiges
left in Mr. L. Prosser of his mighty ancestry were a pronounced stout-
ness about the turn and a **predilection** for little fur hats.[292]

write your own: |

Procrastinate

prO-'kras-t&-"nAt

(Verb) to postpone or delay doing
something without justification
Keyword: grow grass in late

Larry **procrastinated** so long that he had to **grow grass in late** December, after it started snowing.

Gary continued to **procrastinate**, putting his assignment off until it was overdue.

Roughly 50 million taxpayers, or 40 percent of all taxpayers in the nation, **procrastinate** until the last week before filing.[293]

Her out-of- control workspace was making her increasingly inclined to **procrastinate**. She truly believed that if she were more organized, she'd be able to turn out more work, on time, and be more prosperous.[294]

write your own: |

©Solid A, Inc.   http://SolidA.net

Prodigious

pr&-'di-j&s

(Adjective) enormous or extraordinary
Keyword: ditches

In his search for dinosaur bones, the little boy dug several **prodigious ditches**.

She lifted a **prodigious** amount of weight to free the trapped baby from beneath the derailed train.

She founded the nonprofit Ford's Theatre Society, became a **prodigious** fundraiser for the theater's original plays and musicals and produced more than 150 of them herself.[295]

At fifteen he was already winning the Academie Francaise's approving attention for his poems. He was nineteen when his mother died in 1821 and his boyhood experiences would color his whole **prodigious** output of novels, poetry and plays.[296]

write your own: |

Prolific

pr&-'li-fik

(Adjective) productive/ generating a
large quantity of something
Keyword: pro lifter

The **pro lifter** was very **prolific** with over a dozen children.

Theodore Roosevelt and Winston Churchill were two world leaders who were also **prolific** writers, producing dozens of books each.

His current working theory is that an extremely **prolific** female seeded the highly volcanic region with eggs over a period of decades, and the hatched young are reaching young adulthood....[297]

Born and raised in China, where his father was a missionary ... he received the Bronze Star ... and was also a **prolific** playwright [person who writes plays] and the author of a number of treatises on physics.[298]

write your own: |

Propensity

pr&-'pent-s&-tE or pr&-'pen-s&-tE

(Noun) a tendency
Keyword: Pen City

The writer has a **propensity** to vacation in her imaginary **Pen City**, although her friends urged her to get a life and go somewhere real.

The troubling **propensity** of children to choose passive activities, like TV viewing, is one of the reasons leading to an epidemic of obesity.

Everybody has an artist inside. You are born with the **propensity** to create.[299]

There is in each of us a **propensity** to find someone or something outside ourselves to blame when things go wrong. Some organizations elevate this propensity to a commandment: "Thou shalt always find an external agent [factor] to blame."[300]

write your own: |

prO-'zA-ik

(Adjective) dull or lacking interest; ordinary
Keyword: mosaic

The new **mosaic** display at the art museum was **prosaic**, generating little interest because it was so dull and ordinary.

The **prosaic** handbook for Greg's new job put him to sleep every time he read it.

This book exposes all this in the calm, sometimes **prosaic** writing one would expect from an accountant....[301]

[Wagner] began using magnetic-resonance-imaging (MRI) machines and electron microscopes as cameras, magnifying or looking inside objects as **prosaic** as corncobs and as elusive [evanescent] as dividing cells.[302]

write your own:

Provocation

"prä-v&-'kA-sh&n

(Noun) something that provokes one to anger or action
Keyword: lava formation

Mt. Saint Helen's eruption and rising **lava formation** was a **provocation** for locals and tourists to immediately flee the area.

After a week of **provocation** to join the church softball team by his pastor, Jim finally consented.

Disproportionate [out of proportion] rage or anger, overreaction to minor **provocation**, and cynicism are other embodiments [examples] of suppressed [bottled up] emotion.[303]

[He] called Barney "the most compelling, richly imaginative artist to emerge in years," and the exhibition "an inspired benchmark of ambition, scope and forthright **provocation** for art in the new century."[304]

write your own: _____

'prü-d&nt

(Adjective) careful or cautious in a sensible way; frugal

Keyword: prune dent

Sally was **prudent** and moved her car to avoid any "**prune dents**" while they picked the prunes from the tree.

Because people carelessly make expensive purchases they later regret, it is **prudent** to think about such purchases overnight and seek good advice.

The players that have come in this time are hopefully going to be much more **prudent** and will have the past to learn from.[305]

Prudent art-auction houses and dealers are turning increasingly to Holocaust art theft experts... to avoid representing art whose tainted past could render it difficult to sell, or trigger an international public relations disaster.[306]

write your own:

Purport

'p&r-"pOrt or 'p&r-"port

(Verb) to profess or claim to be
(often something you are not)
Keyword: fur port

The French had several **fur ports** along the Mississippi River, and they **purported** to be the best hunters—although the Native Americans were arguably better.

The book **purported** that anyone can get the best bargain by following three easy rules.

The survey—something less than scientific, since its results are based on reader votes—**purports** to show that the Midwest is emerging as a new area of artistic influence.[307]

From the time children are able even to grasp one of these wooden writing sticks [pencil], they use them to take an endless battery of tests that **purport** to measure their current ability and future potential.[308]

write your own: _____

Querulous

'kwer-y&-l&s or 'kwer-&-l&s

(Adjective) complaining or whining
Keyword: hear you less

Because I hate complaining and whining, I often say, "**I hear you less** the more **querulous** you become."

The **querulous** workers could not get anything accomplished because they spent the day complaining.

Other Billboard employees used to surreptitiously [sneakily] pass around e-mails of [his] run-on sentences and over-the-top enthusiasms. He could be **querulous** and difficult to work for.[309]

He must have noted the troubled looks my mother gave me, my father's **querulous** comments, the awkward silences so unexpected between parent and child.[310]

write your own:

©Solid A, Inc.   http://SolidA.net

Quixotic

(Adjective) impractically idealistic
Keyword: quick sock fit

Looking for the **quick sock fit**, the **quixotic** prince asked every girl to try on the sock that was left behind at the palace sock hop.

The project was labeled **quixotic** by the committee, as it seemed too impractical and idealistic.

Begun as a **quixotic** gesture, blowpipes confronting bulldozers, the protests electrified the international environmental movement, leading then Senator Al Gore to describe the Penan as the frontline troops in the battle to save the Earth. But the logging continued.[311]

Some of the unexplained wealth was devoted to laudable [praiseworthy] public works—a modern road was built leading up to the village, for example, and facilities for running water were provided. Other expenditures were more **quixotic**. A tower was built, the Tour Magdala, overlooking the sheer side of the mountain. An opulent country house was constructed....[312]

write your own: |

Raucous

'ro-k&s

(Adjective) rough-sounding/ in a
disorderly and rowdy manner
Keyword: rock

Mike made a **raucous** noise that woke the neighbors by
throwing **rocks** against his friend's window at night.

The room turned **raucous** within minutes after the rowdy
kids arrived for the birthday party.

[Galveston] gained a reputation as a **raucous** hub of illicit
gambling and wide-open sin until the mid-1950s, when Texas
Rangers shut it down and indirectly helped to reinvent the
city as a tourist destination and family resort.[313]

The 25th annual carnival parade was a **raucous** tribute to
Latin culture....[314]

write your own: |

Redundant

ri-'d&n-d&nt

(Adjective) excessive, needless repetition
Keyword: read and dance

She **read and danced** Swan Lake so much that it became **redundant**.

Susan's **redundant** use of the term "cool" became very annoying after she repeated it so often.

At the moment (though not, I hope, by the time you read it), this article is a mess of **redundant**, poorly phrased, haphazardly punctuated drivel [babble].[315]

The wording of this article should avoid **redundant** phraseology such as "amend, alter, add to, or repeal," or "alter or amend," or "amend or in any way change."[316]

write your own: _____

_____

Refurbish

ri-'f&r-bish

(Verb) to make something look new
and bright again; to restore
Keyword: fur dish

The movie star **refurbished** Kitty's **fur dish** with a fresh coat of fur.

The program was approved to **refurbish** the dilapidated art school with paintings and sculptures from local artists.

Other local do-gooders range from Kirk and Anne Douglas, who gave $1 million last year to help **refurbish** 400 Los Angeles County school playgrounds....[317]

The Jockey Club believes in this promise: In the past two years it has plunked down $300 million to **refurbish** its Happy Valley racetrack and to build a gleaming new headquarters.[318]

write your own: _____

218   ©Solid A, Inc.   http://SolidA.net

Relegate

're-l&-"gAt

(Verb) to assign to a particular group or category
(often to a less important rank or position)
Keyword: real low gate

The equestrian rider's poor performance **relegated** him to the easiest course with the **real low gate**.

The stuffed bear, once the little girl's favorite toy, was **relegated** to the "give away box" after she became interested in Barbie dolls.

"Expect the best at all times. Never think of the worst. Drop it out of your thought, **relegate** it. Let there be no thought in your mind that the worst will happen." - Norman Vincent Peale.[319]

Also, watercolor brushes are a lot more expensive than oil brushes, and they don't last as long. When they lose their fine points, I **relegate** them to the lesser tasks of mixing and covering broad areas with washes.[320]

write your own:

Section 8 Crossword Puzzle

©Solid A, Inc.   http://SolidA.net

Across

4. self-important or arrogant

7. likely to be true; believable

8. to assign to a particular group or category (often to a less important rank or position)

9. a tendency

10. to profess or claim to be (often something you are not)

13. careful or cautious in a sensible way; frugal

14. a preconceived liking; a preference for something

15. dull or lacking interest; ordinary

16. yielding; easily manipulated or changed

17. an attack or defense regarding a set of principles, ideals, or opinions; argument; debate; controversy

Down

1. to postpone or delay doing something without justification

2. to make something look new and bright again; to restore

3. complaining or whining

5. very steep

6. excessive, needless repetition

7. enormous or extraordinary

11. rough-sounding; in a disorderly and rowdy manner

12. impractically idealistic

14. productive; generating a large quantity of something

15. something that provokes one to anger or action

Section 8 Multiple Choice Review

Select the word that best fits each sentence.

1. The _____ of patients to bring lawsuits against their doctors has consequently increased the cost of medical care and insurance.
   a. predilection   b. procrastination   c. propensity   d. polemic

2. Patrick quit his job after he was _____ to treasurer from the position of vice president.
   a. procrastinated   b. relegated   c. purported   d. refurbished

3. In her _____ she argued her cased and stated that she would stand by the cause no matter what happened.
   a. polemic   b. propensity   c. profusion   d. provocation

4. Susan's book centers on a(n) _____ character who finds the meaning of life in chivalry. He tries to come to the rescue of nearly anyone, even if it is well beyond his ability or means.
   a. quixotic   b. raucous   c. pliant   d. querulous

5. It is _____ to seek cover in a basement during a tornado warning.
   a. redundant   b. prudent   c. prodigious   d. plausible

6. Matt loves the difficult black diamond ski routes—the more _____ the ski route the better.
   a. plausible   b. pompous   c. precipitous   d. raucous

7. After taking yoga classes for six months, Katrina found that her body was more _____ and she could scratch her nose with her toe.
   a. prolific   b. quixotic   c. prodigious   d. pliant

8. Wyatt acquired a(n) _____ for Mexican food after he spent the summer in Mexico City, and now orders it every chance he gets.
   a. polemic   b. profusion   c. provocation   d. predilection

9. Michael Jordan is one of the most _____ scorers in NBA history.
   a. quixotic   b. prolific   c. precipitous   d. pompous

10. Stop _____ and start working.
   a. procrastinating   b. refurbishing   c. relegating   d. purporting

11. The door-to-door vacuum salesman's speech sounded so _____ that he sold a record number of machines.
   a. prodigious   b. precipitous   c. plausible   d. prosaic

12. The meaning of the word "protected" is _____ in the sentence, "She felt safe and protected in the house."
   a. relegated   b. refurbished   d. prudent   c. redundant

13. His _____ feat of climbing the seven highest mountains in the fastest time was honored with a Guinness World Record.
   a. plausible   b. procrastinating   c. prosaic   d. prodigious

14. The talent show was _____ and failed to hold our interest.
   a. prolific   b. prudent   c. prodigious   d. prosaic

15. The liquid vitamin drink was _____ to contain all of the necessary vitamins the body needs and in the exact proportions.
   a. relegated   b. purported   c. pompous   d. redundant

16. The old playground was _____ with new slides, teeter-totters, monkey bars and merry-go-rounds.
   a. refurbished   b. relegated   c. purported   d. redundant

17. As the woman grew older, she became more _____ and harder to get along with because she complained and whined about everything.
   a. pliant   b. precipitous   c. prolific   d. querulous

18. Due to his _____ voice, people who first meet Chris tend to believe that he is a tough character, but in actuality he is very gentle.
   a. refurbished   b. relegated   c. purported   d. raucous

19. Joseph started acting _____, refusing to play with his old friends, after he received the lead part in the school drama.
   a. prosaic   b. querulous   c. pompous   d. prudent

20. Ignoring his antagonist's _____, Victor turned around and walked away from him.
   a. propensity   b. profusion   c. predilection   d. provocation

Section 8 Matching Review

Match the word on the left to the correct meaning on the right.

1. _____ Plausible
2. _____ Pliant
3. _____ Polemic
4. _____ Pompous
5. _____ Precipitous
6. _____ Predilection
7. _____ Procrastinate
8. _____ Prodigious
9. _____ Prolific
10. _____ Propensity
11. _____ Prosaic
12. _____ Provocation
13. _____ Prudent
14. _____ Purport
15. _____ Querulous
16. _____ Quixotic
17. _____ Raucous
18. _____ Redundant
19. _____ Refurbish
20. _____ Relegate

A. to postpone or delay doing something without justification
B. careful or cautious in a sensible way; frugal
C. likely to be true; believable
D. excessive, needless repetition
E. impractically idealistic
F. an attack or defense regarding a set of principles, ideals, or opinions; argument; debate; controversy
G. dull or lacking interest; ordinary
H. complaining or whining
I. a preconceived liking; a preference for something
J. enormous or extraordinary
K. to assign to a particular group or category (often to a less important rank or position)
L. something that provokes one to anger or action
M. yielding; easily manipulated or changed
N. very steep
O. productive; generating a large quantity of something
P. to make something look new and bright again; to restore
Q. self-important or arrogant
R. a tendency
S. to profess or claim to be (often something you are not)
T. rough-sounding; in a disorderly and rowdy manner

Section Nine

ri-'mors

(Noun) a strong feeling of guilt or regret about past deeds

Keyword: Morse (as in Morse Code)

After sending a false S.O.S. through **Morse Code**, the captain began to feel **remorse** when other ships started coming to his rescue.

Shopping in the same store can cause **remorse** when the same silk shirt purchased last week at full price is now on sale for half.

"Quite frankly, I think Mr. Flores does fall into the category of the worst of the worst," Superior Court Judge ... said as she sentenced a defiant [defendant]. "He has absolutely no **remorse**, as if he has no soul."[321]

It's important in life to conclude things properly. Only then can you let go. Otherwise you are left with words you should have said but never did, and your heart is heavy with **remorse**. That bungled good-bye hurts me to this day.[322]

write your own:

Reprobate

're-pr&-"bAt

(Noun) an immoral, vicious person
Keyword: wreck a date

The **reprobate** was so mean and self-centered that he often **wrecked a date** with one mean comment.

Garrett was labeled a **reprobate** after he was caught beating a bunny.

I practically live on the Internet. Are my life and finances an open book for every intelligent **reprobate** who has a browser?[323]

After several waiting patients averted [turned away] their eyes, he realized he must look like a **reprobate**. He hadn't shaved during their trip and had spent a virtually sleepless night on the train.[324]

write your own: |

Repugnant

ri-'p&g-n&nt

(Adjective) unpleasant; causing disgust
Keyword: pregnant

After tripping in the sewer, the **pregnant** woman smelled **repugnant**.

Discriminating against someone because of his or her race or culture is morally offensive and **repugnant**.

Though hoarders may lead otherwise normal lives, they become accustomed to **repugnant** conditions in their homes caused by having dozens and even hundreds of pets.[325]

The point is that we all find ways to justify morally **repugnant** acts to ourselves.[326]

write your own:

©Solid A, Inc.   http://SolidA.net

Respite

'res-p&t or ri-'spIt

(Noun) a pause or rest
Keyword: rest from spit

The contestants were given a **respite** in the watermelon seed spitting contest, after they asked for a **rest from spitting**.

After peddling thousands of miles across the country, the bicyclists took a short **respite** at the lake, enjoying a lazy afternoon.

It seems impossible to image that there was a time when I looked upon a live sea turtle as a ten-course meal of great delicacy, a blessed **respite** from fish.[327]

However, I think the audience needs a break from the ... course of the play, which begins to feel unstructured as it progresses without **respite**.[328]

write your own: |

Reticent

‘re-t&-s&nt

(Adjective) uncommunicative; tending
to be silent; keeping to oneself
Keyword: rent a tent

Greg liked to keep to himself and decided that in order to remain **reticent** it would be best to **rent a tent** instead of staying in a cabin with his friends.

In police custody, he remained **reticent**, refusing to answer any questions about his whereabouts the previous evening.

But Burris, who isn't the least bit **reticent** to tell the world he isn't happy that the [Green Bay] Packers gave up on him after one season, won't hold back when it comes to providing the Bears staff any tidbit of information that might be used against his former team.[329]

His **reticent** manner was considered ideal for coping with the demands of celebrityhood.[330]

write your own: _____

     http://SolidA.net

Ruthless

'ruth-l&s

Adjective) cruel; showing no mercy
Keyword: toothless

The dentist was **ruthless**, making his patient **toothless** by yanking out his teeth.

In order to win the race, Judy was **ruthless**, pushing and elbowing her opponents.

[She] survived two decades as a soldier in Cambodia's **ruthless** civil war.[331]

Speaking with the utmost conviction, Shackleton pointed out that no article was of any value when weighed against their ultimate survival, and he exhorted them to be **ruthless** in ridding themselves of every unnecessary ounce, regardless of its value. [Excerpt from Sir Ernest Shackleton's epic story of survival in the Antarctic]. [332]

write your own: |

Salient

'sA-ly&nt or 'sA-lE-&nt

(Adjective) highly noticeable, prominent,
or most important
Keyword: sail ants

The **sail ants** were highly **salient** as they sailed their little boat across the bathtub.

Journalism students are required to listen to speeches for the most important information, and then to report the most **salient** points.

Over the course of the last 25 years, Gallup researchers have qualitatively and quantitatively assessed the most **salient** employee perceptions [views] of management practices. Gallup researchers have sought to define a core set of statements that measure important perceptions across a wide spectrum of organizations.[333]

Cell phones won't display the same image as a PC; instead, information will be automatically scaled to best fit each display, preserving the **salient** details.[334]

write **your own:**

http://SolidA.net

Sanctimonious

"sa[ng]k-t&-'mO-nE-&s

(Adjective) acting morally superior; hypocritically pious or devout
Keyword: sank

After his **sanctimonious** comment, "Nothing can sink us," the Titanic **sank**.

The boy's mother was **sanctimonious** around the other parents because she was president of the Parent-Teacher Organization and grand prize winner at the fair's bake-off competition.

He was intellectual but practical, spiritual but not **sanctimonious**, proud but never arrogant.[335]

Now, I [famous actor Sidney Poitier] couldn't tell him at the time, and maybe it'll sound a little **sanctimonious** even now, after all these years, but I rejected that part because, in my view, the character simply didn't measure up.[336]

write your own: |

Scapegoat

'skAp-"gOt

(Noun) one who bears blame for others
Keyword: escaped goat

He became the **scapegoat** for the **escaped goat** while his friend fled the scene to avoid getting in trouble.

Unwilling to take the blame themselves for writing graffiti on the walls, the children made Fred their **scapegoat**.

Parents get so angry and frustrated that they lash out, not only at the child but at each other. Soon full-scale battles erupt as the child becomes the **scapegoat** for everything that's wrong in the family.[337]

One of the Web's cherished myths, that advertising will pay for content, is rapidly crumbling as one ad-supported site after another expires. One handy **scapegoat** in all this is the ubiquitous [widespread] "ad banner," which usually appears at the top of a Web page.[338]

write your own: |

Seminal

'se-m&-n&l

(Adjective) origin, or the beginning of something (often influencing later developments)
Keyword: cement ball

Some say the **seminal** beginning to the modern game of basketball originated with the Aztecs who played a similar game with a hard rubber ball that felt rather like a **cement ball**.

The **seminal** game "Pong," regarded by many as the first video game, may be credited for starting a new genre in entertainment.

[His] **seminal** work has made him a contender ... for a Nobel Prize.[339]

He played trombone and guitar with his brothers and cousins before hitting the road and embarking [starting] on a career that would lead him to such **seminal** jazz groups as the Count Basie Orchestra and the Bennie Moten band.[340]

write your own:

Sententious

sen-'tent-sh&s or sen-'ten-sh&s

(Adjective) short and full of meaning;
excessive moralizing
Keyword: sentence

The old **sententious** saying, "A good name endures forever,"
is a **sentence** valid for us today.

The professor was known for quoting **sententious** sayings
in his excessively moralistic lectures.

He can be old and miserable when work is going badly, or
old and **sententious** when it's going well....[341]

Remember the proverb, nothing ventured nothing gained.
Persuaded by these **sententious** words, one of the blind men
let go of the rope and went, with arms outstretched, in the
direction of the uproar.[342]

write your own:

Serene

s&-'rEn

(Adjective) calm, tranquil, or pleasant
Keyword: siren

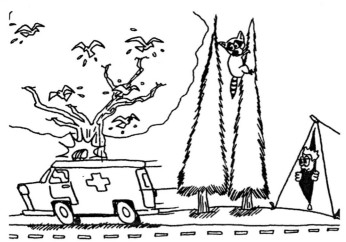

The ambulance's **siren** ruined the **serene** effect of the quiet wilderness camp.

Yoga is a **serene** exercise that focuses on deep breathing and creating a clear mind.

With these and other simple measures, he promises, "the fussiest babies can be made very calm, and the calmest babies can be made absolutely **serene**."[343]

For now, given its size, [Istanbul] is remarkably **serene** and safe—I have often seen men counting big wads of money in public without fear of being attacked and robbed.[344]

write your own: |

Sophomoric

"säf-'mOr-ik or "säf-'mor-ik

(Adjective) overconfident about thinking one knows
something one actually knows little about; immature
Keyword: sophomore

Because the **sophomore** student acted silly and **sophomoric** in class, he was temporarily kicked out until he could be more mature.

On the last day of school the students acted silly and **sophomoric** which caused their teacher to cut their party short.

Even these well-cast actors can't disguise the **sophomoric**, sitcom-inspired nature of so much of the writing.[345]

The Man Show, the **sophomoric** variety show on Comedy Central, was an obvious choice for the [advertising] spots.[346]

write your own:

Soporific

"sä-p&-'ri-fik

(Adjective) causing sleep or drowsiness
Keyword: Soap Terrific

Soap Terrific contains a **soporific** ingredient that tends to make people sleepy.

The slow, repetitive beat of the music had a **soporific** effect on the audience, causing many people to fall asleep.

Overstimulated folk used to be sent to relax in the **soporific** climate of Bournemouth [England].[347]

I think Reza believes our culture has made us all so numb with constant media bombardment that ordinary theatre has a **soporific** quality. I think you have to get right up in people's face and scream at them, if not vocally, with images.[348]

write your own: _____

Spurious

'spyur-E-&s

(Adjective) false; not valid

Keyword: spur

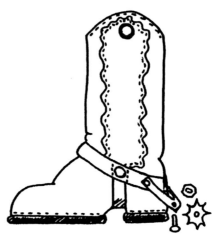

The **spurious spur** fell apart because it was made of cheap plastic.

The scientific data proving the theory turned out to be **spurious**—fabricated by scientists who were willing to falsify their research in return for money.

I quit my job and began to support myself on the proceeds of my **spurious** checks. I didn't keep track of the number of bum checks I passed, but my standard of living improved remarkably... After two months of cranking out worthless checks, however, I faced myself with some unpleasant truths. I was a crook.[349]

In 1996, InfoGlide discovered a new market. Fraud rings were costing the insurance industry hundreds of millions of dollars in **spurious** claims each year.[350]

write your own: |

©Solid A, Inc. http://SolidA.net

Squalid

'skwä-l&d

(Adjective) extremely dirty, often because of poverty or neglect
Keyword: squid

SQUID TANK

The water in the **squid** tank was **squalid** because the zookeeper was neglectful and rarely cleaned it.

The refugees lived in a **squalid**, makeshift camp of cardboard boxes and tires.

The closest thing we had to a diner was a place down by the Raccoon River called Ernie's Grill. Everything about it was **squalid** and greasy, including Ernie, and the food was appalling....[351]

When they are not traveling or training elsewhere, both of them live in Volgograd [Russia], a sprawling, **squalid** city of one million that was once called Stalingrad.[352]

write your own: _____

Stringent

'strin-j&nt

(Adjective) imposing strict standards
Keyword: string net

Fishermen are very **stringent** about repairing their **string nets** exactly right.

The new teacher is more **stringent** with a set of rules for nearly any conceivable infraction.

During 2 1/2 stormy years as the nation's top environmental regulator, Whitman was widely seen as the administration's leading advocate for **stringent** clean air and water rules.[353]

The child with ADD [Attention Deficit Disorder] chronically fails to meet obligations, do chores, stay up with schoolwork, keep to family schedules ... and in general "get with the program" at home. This leads to chronic limit-setting by parents, with increasingly **stringent** penalties and increasingly tight limitations on the child.[354]

write your own:

Succinct

"s&k-'si[ng]kt or s&-'si[ng]t

(Adjective) brief and clear
Keyword: sub sink

The newspaper was very **succinct** in its article, "Did the **sub sink**?"

The editor rejected the lengthy story for publication because it was not **succinct** and failed to get to the point.

With spirited kids who are taking in everything around them, we too can only expect to catch their attention for a few seconds. That means our messages need to be **succinct** and to the point: Stop! Bed. Shoes. Eat. Come.[355]

These are all attempts to articulate, in a **succinct** way, the essence of something for which to aim, and something that actually could be attained with effort.[356]

write your own:

Supercilious

'sü-p&r-'si-lE-&s or 'sü-p&r-'sil-y&s

(Adjective) haughty, conceited, or putting others down
Keyword: super silly

The conceited and **supercilious** professor thought he was too good for the school, but his students thought he looked **super silly**.

The author read an excerpt from his novel in a **supercilious** tone, as though he was reading from the most important document ever written.

It is remarkable to meet a famous person who you expect to be arrogant or **supercilious**, only to encounter self-deprecation [belittling or disparaging oneself] and shyness instead.[357]

The photo shows Peter outside his mansion, wearing an unbelievably **supercilious** expression....[358]

write your own:

©Solid A, Inc.　　　　http://SolidA.net

Superfluous

su-'p&r-flü-&s

(Adjective) extra; exceeding the necessary amount
Keyword: super floss

The government's **superfluous** spending on **super floss** for the Statue of Liberty was unnecessary.

The teacher crossed out the **superfluous** words in the students' essays to illustrate how to write more concisely.

I think my biggest strength, at least the strength that will have the biggest impact on our success, is my ability to see through fluffy, **superfluous** information and cut to the point that matters. I have a way of eliminating unnecessary details and getting to the heart of an issue....[359]

Which brings us to Cassandra Wilson. I mean Cassandra: Fame has rendered the last name **superfluous**....[360]

write your own: |

Section 9 Crossword Puzzle

    http://SolidA.net

Across

1. false; not valid

4. extra; exceeding the necessary amount

5. highly noticeable, prominent, or most important

6. overconfident about thinking one knows something one actu ally knows little about; immature

9. cruel; showing no mercy

10. a strong feeling of guilt or regret about past deeds

11. short and full of meaning/ excessive moralizing

14. acting morally superior

16. imposing strict standards

Down

2. extremely dirty, often because of poverty or neglect

3. haughty, conceited, or putting others down

4. causing sleep or drowsiness

5. one who bears blame for others

7. a pause or rest

8. origin; the beginning of something (often influencing later developments)

9. unpleasant; causing disgust

10. uncommunicative; tending to be silent; keeping to oneself

12. an immoral, vicious person

13. brief and clear

15. calm, tranquil, or pleasant

Section 9 Multiple Choice Review

Select the word that best fits each sentence.

1. The professor's _____ tone of voice during the slide show lulled a majority of the students to sleep.
   a. repugnant   b. seminal   c. superfluous   d. soporific

2. The coach's short message to the team was _____ and the players knew precisely what they needed to do to make a come back in the game.
   a. stringent   b. reticent   c. ruthless   d. succinct

3. Erin acted _____ around her colleagues after receiving the academic scholarship.
   a. serene   b. sanctimonious   c. superfluous   d. sophomoric

4. The teenage _____ was considered both mean and immoral, and appeared to be on a fast track to prison.
   a. scapegoat   b. remorse   c. respite   d. reprobate

5. Charlie did not want to talk about his past and remained _____.
   a. reticent   b. ruthless   c. sententious   d. sanctimonious

6. When hiking, I try to avoid packing _____ clothing in order to travel lightly.
   a. repugnant   b. seminal   c. superfluous   d. supercilious

7. After fighting with her best friend, she felt great _____ and wanted to apologize.
   a. repugnance   b. remorse   c. reticence   d. respite

8. Knowing his defense was not too strong; the lawyer skirted the _____ facts of the case and attempted to focus on smaller details.
   a. succinct   b. seminal   c. salient   d. supercilious

9. Although she had nothing to do with the broken window, Sally was made the _____ by the guilty children.
   a. reprobate   b. respite   c. scapegoat   d. sophomore

10. His speech used many _____ quotes that expressed a lot of meaning in just a few words.
a. sententious   b. spurious   c. sanctimonious   d. salient

11. She acts _____ and regularly puts others down.
a. supercilious   b. soporific   c. remorse   d. reticent

12. As the first scientist to study the topic, Dr. Tony Smith was especially pleased to see his _____ work published.
a. spurious   b. superfluous   c. succinct   d. seminal

13. Hurting other players to win at all costs is a _____ attitude of some athletes.
a. reticent   b. salient   c. soporific   d. repugnant

14. Despite all of the trouble around him, he remained _____ and relaxed.
a. reticent   b. serene   c. sententious   d. supercilious

15. Wanting to gain attention, Angela pretended to have a boyfriend by writing several _____ love letters to herself and then reading them aloud to all of her friends.
a. spurious   b. sententious   c. soporific   d. supercilious

16. With people as _____ as Mike, who needs enemies?
a. sententious   b. squalid   c. stringent   d. ruthless

17. Even under the most _____ circumstances, the homeless children found joy in imaginative play.
a. remorse   b. squalid   c. salient   d. superfluous

18. The new radio personality's _____ views turned many of the station's normal listeners off.
a. succinct   b. stringent   c. sophomoric   d. squalid

19. The counselor recommended the young rebellious boy join the army because he needed more _____ guidelines and discipline.
a. ruthless   b. spurious   c. stringent   d. serene

20. After working hours without any breaks, Jill was badly in need of a _____.
a. scapegoat   b. reprobate   c. respite   d. remorse

Section 9 Matching Review

Match the word on the left to the correct meaning on the right.

1. _____ Remorse
2. _____ Reprobate
3. _____ Repugnant
4. _____ Respite
5. _____ Reticent
6. _____ Ruthless
7. _____ Salient
8. _____ Sanctimonious
9. _____ Scapegoat
10. _____ Seminal
11. _____ Sententious
12. _____ Serene
13. _____ Sophomoric
14. _____ Soporific
15. _____ Spurious
16. _____ Squalid
17. _____ Stringent
18. _____ Succinct
19. _____ Supercilious
20. _____ Superfluous

A. short and full of meaning/ excessive moralizing
B. extra; exceeding the necessary amount
C. imposing strict standards
D. a strong feeling of guilt or regret about past deeds
E. brief and clear
F. an immoral, vicious person
G. a pause or rest
H. unpleasant; causing disgust
I. origin; the beginning of something (often influencing later developments)
J. cruel; showing no mercy
K. highly noticeable, prominent, or most important
L. one who bears blame for others
M. overconfident about thinking one knows something one actually knows little about; immature
N. false; not valid
O. uncommunicative; tending to be silent; keeping to oneself
P. causing sleep or drowsiness
Q. acting morally superior
R. calm, tranquil, or pleasant
S. haughty; conceited; putting others down
T. extremely dirty, often because of poverty or neglect

Section Ten

Tactless

(Adjective) not showing sensitivity in dealing with others

Keyword: tack

The teacher scolded the student for being **tactless** when he left a **tack** on the chair.

It was rather **tactless** of Jim to ask his ex-girlfriend to join him and his new girlfriend on a date.

But not only is it tasteless and **tactless** to point out that there is money to be made out of war and suffering, it is also dangerous to assume that defense companies are flourishing [prospering].[361]

Burly, blunt, often **tactless** and profane, with a face that might be described as "40 miles of bad road," he chain-smoked Old Golds, drank too much and too often, and sometimes vanished into an alcoholic void.[362]

write your own:

Tawdry

'to-drE or 'tä-drE

(Adjective) cheap; showy in a tasteless way; gaudy
Keyword: tall tree

The Christmas ornaments on the **tall tree** looked rather **tawdry**, as if they were purchased at a five and dime store.

The actress's gown looked glamorous onscreen, however its sequins and gems looked plastic and **tawdry** up close.

The Group's focus on the urban underbelly [the city's corrupt area], and its emphasis on the life-styles of ordinary, working class Londoners in a run-down, **tawdry** area, had a resounding impact.[363]

Somewhere in Australia, an auto-sales company is using a **tawdry** Audrey Hepburn lookalike—in TV and print ads....[364]

write your own: |

Temerity

t&-'mer-&-tE

(Noun) nerve; recklessness; boldness arising from contempt of danger or opposition

Keyword: to marry

With great **temerity** the boy decided **to marry** his girlfriend even though her mobster father vehemently opposed it.

Larry had the **temerity** to rebel against his teacher, even though he knew it could mean the loss of his recesses.

However, he could see that Mother was right: the king might believe, or pretend to believe, that no one could have the **temerity** to rebel against him....[365]

A criminal lawyer, Nouman had the **temerity** to defend a man Uday wanted punished for insulting his girlfriend, and Nouman paid for it with nearly two decades' worth of torment....[366]

write your own: |

   http://SolidA.net

Tenacity

t&-'na-s&-tE

(Noun) extreme persistence or determination
Keyword: ten cities

Sean demonstrated great **tenacity**, running nonstop to **ten cities**.

With many hurdles to overcome and miles to endure, her **tenacity** helped her to win the triathlon.

Witt describes the heroism and the **tenacity** of Americans who survive the worst and recover against the greatest odds.[367]

And then there was Lee Iacocca, who had his back to the wall, painted into a corner and hanging by his fingernails, among other metaphoric travails—a regular industrial Indiana Jones. But he led Chrysler from the Temple of Doom, and his struggle demonstrated what can be achieved with talent and **tenacity**.[368]

write your own:

Tentative

'ten-t&-tiv

(Adjective) not certain/ plan or idea
not fully developed/ experimental
Keyword: tent

After putting up the **tent**, they realized that their plans to go camping looked **tentative** with the oncoming storm.

The workers made a **tentative** deal with the company that would temporarily improve the working conditions until a new, safer building could be constructed.

MetroWest Medical Center employees ... have reached a **tentative** agreement with the hospital that includes wage increases and improvements in working conditions.....[369]

Although the networks have not locked down their schedules yet, they are quietly telling buyers about **tentative** plans.[370]

write your own:

©Solid A, Inc.   http://SolidA.net

Terse

't&rs

(Adjective) concise or brief
Keyword: verse

"Jesus wept" is the **tersest verse** in the Bible with only two words.

The ship's crew immediately obeyed the **terse** orders of the captain without asking for further explanation.

He had a pregame meeting with Frank Thomas to discuss **terse** comments the two made after Sunday's game in Seattle.[371]

Let's create a process of information digestion in which inexpensive data are gathered from largely open sources and condensed, through an open process, into knowledge **terse** and insightful enough to inspire wisdom in our leaders.[372]

write your own:

Threadbare

'thred-"bar

(Adjective) shabby, tattered, or worn thin
Keyword: red bear

Color threadbare
sweater red

The **red bear's** favorite shirt was **threadbare**.

Sam wore his favorite shirt so often that it became **threadbare** beyond repair.

The paradox was poverty amid plenty, certain evidence that the usual system of matching consumers with producers had gone awry. While millions of Americans wore **threadbare** clothes, 13 million bales of cotton went unsold. As reports of malnourished children soared, food rotted in fields and orchards.[373]

I wore my patched, thin, and **threadbare** navy surplus shirt and my equally worn navy surplus gabardine trousers: the remains of the clothes I had on when they picked me up.[374]

write your own: |

258   ©Solid A, Inc.   http://SolidA.net

Undermine

'&n-d&r-'mIn

(Verb) to weaken (especially someone's power or chances of success) gradually or secretly
Keyword: under the mine

The request for safety equipment for the tunnel **under the mine** was **undermined** by the mayor in order to save money.

Sandy's lack of confidence in speaking in front of the class was further **undermined** when she spotted a couple of students giggling while she spoke.

We spent far too much time finding fault with one another, much to the delight of our enemies, who were content to watch us **undermine** our own case rather than undermining theirs.[375]

The airline said yesterday that if Heathrow, the world's busiest international airport, were to be ignored in plans for increased airport capacity in southeast England, it would restrict UK [United Kingdom] economic development. It would also **undermine** London's position as an international aviation hub and put its position as Europe's leading city at risk.[376]

write your own: |

Ungainly

"&n-'gAn-lE

(Adjective) awkward or clumsy
Keyword: game

His **ungainly** manners during the **game** upset the other player.

The model's **ungainly** strut down the walkway seemed strangely unfitting and awkward.

Her mood was not improved by the baby she carried, which made her **ungainly** and nothing like the graceful lady of the house she felt herself to be.[377]

The only real complaint that can be leveled against the book's production is that the print is unjustified-that is, the lines do not all end at the same point on the page, which creates **ungainly** and irritating serration [uneven margin].[378]

write your own:

©Solid A, Inc.   http://SolidA.net

Unscathed

"&n-'skA[th]d

(Adjective) without harm or injury
Keyword: skate

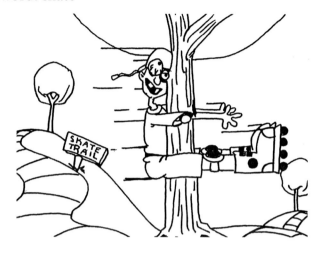

Poor Jimmy never seems to **skate unscathed** and returns with bruises all over his body.

Although many people were badly hurt, Dorothy was left **unscathed** by the accident.

It started as a typical journey until Chuck rounded a corner, skidded on some ice and crashed his bike. Chuck rose from the wreck **unscathed**—his only mar was a few holes in the sleeve of his sweatshirt....[379]

How rare it is for the nuance [meaning and feeling] of written fiction to make it **unscathed** when transformed to film or television.[380]

write your own:

Vacillate

'va-s&-"lAt

(Verb) to fluctuate between opposing ideas; to waver

Keyword: Vaseline

With so many types of **Vaseline** available, he was unable to make up his mind and **vacillated** between his choices.

Kristi **vacillated** about whether or not to purchase the dress for weeks until it was no longer available.

We **vacillate** and fluctuate. How we feel about our decisions—even the way we make them—changes from day to day.[381]

She found herself starting to question, waiver, doubt, and **vacillate**.[382]

write your own: |

Validate

'va-l&-"dAt

(Verb) to approve; to confirm; to verify
Keyword: valley date

ARE WE STILL ON FOR THE VALLEY DATE?

OF COURSE.

He **validated** their **valley date** by personally meeting with her to be sure she had not forgotten.

He felt he could have written the book on child-rearing as it **validated** nearly every one of his ideas about how to raise children.

He is also asked to **validate** her feelings—to let her know he considers them legitimate, that he respects and empathizes with her even if he doesn't share her perspective.[383]

Responding to the Impressionist (and later, Cubist) movement in Europe, American artists sought to **validate** their work by recognizing and adopting the methods of their European counterparts, but also to distinguish themselves as American artists.[384]

write your own: _____

Venerate

've-n&-"rAt

(Verb) to regard or respect highly
Keyword: vender's rates

Although his prices were high, everyone **venerated** the **vender's rates** because his food was regarded so highly.

The World War II Memorial Park was created to **venerate** those who fought and died for their country.

They believe that their teacher must be a much wiser and more advanced person, so they think they should imitate him and do what he says without question and **venerate** him as a model of perfect wisdom.[385]

For decades a state propaganda machine [agency used for spreading ideas] served up ideological poster children for the masses to **venerate**.[386]

write your own:

Viable

'vI-&-b&l

(Adjective) workable; practical; able to succeed/
 capable of living
Keyword: Bible

The **Bible** gives many **viable** principles for living.

Building a large luxury hotel was not a **viable** idea for the very small town with few tourists.

Find situations that need fixing, come up with several **viable** solutions, and then take them to a leader with good problem-solving experience.[387]

While on campus he trained with the Aztecs' track team and mulled over his options, the most **viable** of which appeared to be a $40,000 offer to work at Teledyne....[388]

write your own: _____

_____

Volatile

'vä-l&-t[&]l

(Adjective) changing suddenly or unexpectedly/
sudden, explosive violence
Keyword: Volley Tile

No one gets to play **Volley Tile** twice, a **volatile** game where people volley explosives over tiles.

The **volatile** stock market often fluctuates hundreds of points each day.

"A change in the pattern of geyser eruptions might also be taken as a clue, he said, but these too vary unpredictably.... If [the geyser] blew today and again next week, that wouldn't tell us anything at all about what it might do the following week or the week after or twenty years from now," Doss says. "The whole park is so **volatile** that it's essentially impossible to draw conclusions from almost anything...."[389]

Toddlers who were rated as "undercontrolled" (irritable, impulsive, and emotionally **volatile**) were twice as likely to be involved in risky behaviors almost two decades later.[390]

write your own: |

Voluminous

v&-'lü-m&-n&s

(Adjective) having a large volume, size or number
(often describing cloth or writing)
Keyword: volume

The prolific author's **voluminous** stories were published in
several **volumes.**

The bride's gown was made of so much silk fabric that she
needed several bridesmaids to hold the **voluminous** train
that trailed behind.

Most companies happily depend on underground fiber-optic
lines for the high-speed transmission of **voluminous** data.[391]

Several years ago, the ever-industrious Erwitt realized that
his **voluminous** photo files held hundreds of pictures of
dogs—alone and with people—many shot at pooch level and
inviting amusing comparison of master and beast.[392]

write your own: |

Waive

'wАv

(Verb) to postpone/ to voluntarily give up something

Keyword: wave

Before / After

In court, Larry **waived** his right to an attorney. The next day he was **waving** to us from jail.

To attract more shoppers, normal parking fees were **waived** during the holiday season.

Based on my experience and based on some conversations with IRS [Internal Revenue Service] appeals officers, you may be able to get the IRS to **waive** penalties if you relied on a bad answer from these people.[393]

During the French presidential election, the candidates proposed that the government **waive** the payroll taxes of any company that phased down to a 30-hour week.[394]

write your own:

©Solid A, Inc.   http://SolidA.net

Wanton

'won-t&n or 'wän-t&n

(Adjective) showing extreme lack of care or control
Keyword: one ton

Because of her **wanton** eating habits, she weighed at least **one ton**.

His drunk driving shows a **wanton** disregard for the safety of his passengers and others on the road.

By Berst's estimate, 10% of the member schools are **wanton** cheaters.[395]

But don't think the **wanton** destruction of the rain forest is going to end next week.[396]

write your own:

'hwet or 'wet

(Verb) to give a small sample of something; to increase one's interest; to stimulate

Keyword: wet

The slice of the **wet** juicy watermelon **whet** the boy's appetite, making him want more.

Their first parachute jump was so exciting that it **whet** their desire for more.

An introductory survey might even **whet** your appetite for more advanced courses....[397]

Only the triumph of his first great discovery remained, to **whet** the imaginations of future treasure hunters.[398]

write your own: |

Zany

‘zA-nE

(Adjective) strangely comical, absurd, or
given to outlandish behavior
Keyword: rainy

He gets **zany** and acts silly when it's **rainy**.

Kosmos Kramer is a **zany** character who generally acts in
unexpected, crazy ways.

If Barry Zito got that haircut—it would mark a **zany** cel-
ebration of the team's hang-loose attitude.[399]

Internet stocks were rocketing skyward like rapid-fire mis-
sile launches; almost anyone with a Web-related idea, no
matter how **zany** (ever hear of Bunions.com?), could raise
millions....[400]

write your own:

Section 10 Crossword Puzzle

©Solid A, Inc.   http://SolidA.net

Across

3. capable of living/ workable; practical; able to succeed

6. cheap; showy in a tasteless way; gaudy

8. nerve; recklessness; boldness arising from contempt of danger or opposition

9. to regard or respect highly

11. to postpone/ to voluntarily give up something

15. showing extreme lack of care or control

16. awkward or clumsy

17. extreme persistence or determination

18. changing suddenly or unexpectedly/ sudden, explosive violence

19. shabby, tattered, or worn thin

Down

1. to approve; to confirm; to verify

2. to weaken (especially someone's power or chances of success) gradually or secretly

4. strangely comical; absurd; given to outlandish behavior

5. concise or brief

7. to give a small sample of something; to increase one's interest; to stimulate

10. not certain/ plan or idea not fully developed/ experimental

12. to fluctuate between opposing ideas; to waver

13. having a large volume, size or number (often describing cloth or writing)

14. without harm or injury

17. not showing sensitivity in dealing with others

Section 10 Multiple Choice Review

Select the word that best fits each sentence.

1. Reader's Digest contains book excerpts that often serve to _____ readers' appetite for the complete story.
   a. waive   b. venerate   c. undermine   d. whet

2. The mother was upset with the _____ happy meal toy and explained to her child that this was a cheap and worthless toy.
   a. viable   b. wanton   c. tawdry   d. tactless

3. The homeless man was draped in over-sized _____ clothes badly in need of repair.
   a. ungainly   b. unscathed   c. zany   d. threadbare

4. The skier's mistakes and _____ performance took him out of the final competition.
   a. ungainly   b. unscathed   c. vacillated   d. venerated

5. In his _____ speech, he managed to embarrass nearly every-one in the audience.
   a. tawdry   b. tactless   c. zany   d. voluminous

6. In need of more applications, the college decided to _____ the deadline for another week.
   a. undermine   b. whet   c. waive   d. vacillate

7. In the face of risking her job, she had the _____ to ask her boss for a raise.
   a. temerity   b. tenacity   c. veneration   d. validation

8. Her mood _____ from one extreme to the other; one day she seems like the nicest person on the planet and the next she is grumpy and continually complaining.
   a. waives   b. validates   c. vacillates   d. venerates

9. The discovery of a complete Stenonychosaurus skeleton _____ the former theory that this dinosaur bore some resemblance to man.
   a. waived   b. undermined   c. unscathed   d. vacillated

10. Uncertain about our summer schedule, we made _____ plans to vacation in New York.
   a. volatile   b. wanton   c. terse   d. tentative

11. Fortunately our home was left _____ by the tornado. Not even a branch was knocked down in our yard.
   a. whet   b. waived   c. unscathed   d. undermined

12. After the second plane crash, people began to question whether the company was still a _____ airline.
   a. viable   b. wanton   c. tawdry   d. tenacious

13. Rather than appreciating herself for who she is, Jane looked to other people in order to feel _____.
   a. validated   b. voluminous   c. tactless   d. volatile

14. Mother Theresa is _____ worldwide for her charitable work with the sick and poor.
   a. undermined   b. validated   c. vacillated   d. venerated

15. Christopher loves _____ clothes that are usually florescent and somewhat mismatched.
   a. threadbare   b. zany   c. tactless   d. ungainly

16. Trying to make fast money, the _____ slum lords continued to rent apartment units that failed to meet any safety standards.
   a. terse   b. threadbare   c. tawdry   d. wanton

17. Everyone around her is careful not to spark her _____ temper.
   a. tentative   b. terse   c. whet   d. volatile

18. Four-year-old Dylan is always watching ants, impressed at their _____ and persistence in getting around any object he put in their way.
   a. temerity   b. veneration   c. tenacity   d. validation

19. When Bob decided to put his life into words, no one thought it would turn into a _____ story several hundred pages long.
   a. tenacious   b. voluminous   c. threadbare   d. ungainly

20. The newspaper editorial drew several _____ replies from readers, briefly stating that they did not agree.
   a. zany   b. terse   c. tawdry   d. threadbare

Section 10 Matching Review

Match the word on the left to the correct meaning on the right.

1. _____ Tactless
2. _____ Tawdry
3. _____ Temerity
4. _____ Tenacity
5. _____ Tentative
6. _____ Terse
7. _____ Threadbare
8. _____ Undermine
9. _____ Ungainly
10. _____ Unscathed
11. _____ Vacillate
12. _____ Validate
13. _____ Venerate
14. _____ Viable
15. _____ Volatile
16. _____ Voluminous
17. _____ Waive
18. _____ Wanton
19. _____ Whet
20. _____ Zany

A. changing suddenly or unexpect edly/ sudden, explosive violence
B. extreme persistence or determina- tion
C. strangely comical; absurd; given to outlandish behavior
D. having a large volume, size or number (often describing cloth or writing)
E. to give a small sample of some thing; to increase one's interest; to stimulate
F. nerve; recklessness; boldness arising from contempt of danger or opposition
G. to postpone; to voluntarily give up something
H. shabby, tattered, or worn thin
I. concise or brief
J. to weaken (especially someone's power or chances of success) gradually or secretly
K. to regard or respect highly
L. not certain/ plan or idea not fully developed/ experimental
M. cheap; showy in a tasteless way; gaudy
N. to fluctuate between opposing ideas; to waver
O. awkward or clumsy
P. to approve; to confirm; to verify
Q. not showing sensitivity in dealing with others
R. without harm or injury
S. showing extreme lack of care or control
T. capable of living/ workable; practi- cal; able to succeed

Free Resources

Free Resources @ www.solida.net

Audio Recordings

 Eliminate the worry of mispronouncing the words by listening to the online audio recordings .

Cartoon Animations

Watch select words from this book come to life in funny and memorable cartoon animations which are sure to make you smile.

Templates

Print or download the "Create Your Own" template to create your own VOCABBUSTERS for your own words.

Learning Style Assessment

Find out more about your learning or cognitive style by taking a free online assessment.

Vocabulary Resources

Discover other great free vocabulary and educational resources and links for teachers, parents and students which can also be accessed at this site.

Need more VOCABBUSTERS words?

Check out VOCABBUSTERS Vol. 1!

Create Your Own

Word: _____

Defintion: _____

_____

```
┌─────────────────────────────────────────────────┐
│                                                   │
│                                                   │
│                                                   │
│                                                   │
│                                                   │
│                                                   │
│                                                   │
│                                                   │
│                                                   │
│                                                   │
└─────────────────────────────────────────────────┘
```

Caption: _____

_____

Example Sentence: _____

_____

_____

_____

For a free downlad of this template, go to http://www.solida.net.

Example Sentence References

1. Bell, M. (2002, February 15). Bowl reopens with bubbly and fanfares. *The Australian*, p. 17.[1]
2. Berry, J. (2003). *The Influentials: One American in Ten Tells the Other Nine How to Vote, Where to Eat, and What to Buy.* New York: Simon and Schuster, Inc., p. 99.[2]
3. Lieberman, D. J. (1998). *Never Be Lied To Again: How to Get the Truth in 5 Minutes or Less in any Conversation or Situation.* New York: St. Martin's Press, p. 77.[3]
4. Walsh, K. T. & Whitelaw, K. (2003, January 20). The year of living dangerously. *U.S. News and World Report*, p. 16.[4]
5. Mitchard, J. (2000, April 30). Sad case, but not grounds for a legal case. *Milwaukee Journal Sentinel*. Retrieved December 22, 2003, from JSOnline http://www.jsonline.com/lifestyle/advice/apr00/mitccol30042900a.asp[5]
6. Kluger, R. (1992, March 30). The sheriff of Nottingham. *People Weekly, 37*, 34.[6]
7. Feedback. (2002, August 10). *New Scientist, 175*, 96.[7]
8. Bryson, B. (2003). *A Short History of Nearly Everything.* New York: Random House, Inc., p. 32.[8]
9. Hernandez, N. (2003, May 15). "What an [expletive] thing to say"... to Ted Turner. *The Washington Post*, p. T02.[9]
10. Collins, Jim (2001). *Good to Great: Why Some Companies Make the Leap... and Others Don't.* New York: HarperCollins Publishers, p.36. [10]
11. Morton, A. (1998). *Diana: Her True Story in her Own Words.* New York: Simon and Schuster, Inc., p. 366.[11]
12. Pryor, K. (1999). *Don't Shoot the Dog! The New Art of Teaching and Training*, New York: Bantom Books, p. 80.[12]
13. Bergant, D. (2003, May 19). What's love got to do with it? *America, 188*, 30.[13]
14. Rosenthal, K. (2001, October 22). Inside dish. *The Sporting News*, p. 12.[14]
15. Valdmanis, T. (2003, March 5). Quattrone quits CSFB to focus on defense. *USA Today*, p. 2B.[15]
16. Stone, D. (2000). *Difficult Conversations: How to Discuss what Matters Most.* New York: Penguin Group, p. 39.[16]
17. Internet stuck in libel web. (2002, December 11). *Australian Financial Review*, p. 54.[17]
18. Bryson, Bill (2003). *A Short History of Nearly Everything.* Broadway Books: USA, p. 145. [18]
19. Hughes, M. (2001, June 21). One fish, two fish. The Dallas World Aquarium makes a great oasis from the summer heat. *Dallas Observer*.[19]
20. Eldredge, J. (2003). *Waking the Dead: The Glory of a Heart Fully Alive.* Nashville, TN: Thomas Nelson, Inc., p. 7.[20]
21. SerVaas, C. (1994, July-August). The Post investigates B12 deficiency. *Saturday Evening Post, 266*, 48-54.[21]
22. Castanon, R. (2003, May 25). Unhappy citizens have own lobbyist. *San Antonio Express-News*, p. 4H.[22]
23. Hare, J. (2002, December). Surviving the Sahara: hypnotic sands, freezing winds ... camels weak from hunger ... evil spirits and an explorer's shadow ... Not your normal winter getaway. *National Geographic, 202*, 54-78.[23]
24. Schutze, J. (2002, August 22). Crossing division street. How do white people learn what to think about race? It's best not to think about it. *Dallas Observer*. Retrieved December 18, 2003, from http://www.dallasobserver.com/issues/2002-08-22/feature.html/1/index.html.[24]
25. Nash, M. (2003, February 3). Cracking the ice: Antarctica is a vast, frozen mystery. Is it thawing, threatening coastal cities? Or is it, in fact, freezing? What scientists have learned. *Time, 161*, 50.[25]
26. Naudi, J. (2003, May 29). Building relationships. *St. Louis Post-Dispatch*, p. C1.[26]

27. Ambrose, S. (1996). *Undaunted Courage: Meriwether Lewis Thomas Jefferson and the Opening of the American West.* New York: Touchstone, p. 32.[27]

28. Isherwood, C. (2000, November 27). Kit Marlowe. *Variety, 381,* 29.[28]

29. Cave, Stephanie and Mitchell, Deborah (2001). *What Your Doctor May Not Tell You About Children's Vaccinations.* New York: Warner Books, p. 13. [29]

30. McWilliams, B. (2001, August 4). Summer sunlight sizzles urban dwellers. *The Irish Times,* City Edition, p. 24.[30]

31. For the record. (2002, December 17). *The Boston Globe,* p. C23.[31]

32. Covey, Stephen M.R., Merrill, Rebecca, and Covey, Stephen R. (2006). *The Speed of Trust: The One Thing that Changes Everything.* New York: Free Press, p. 166. [32]

33. Top 10; Sports stories in the metro area. (1999, December 31). *Times-Picayune,* p. D10.[33]

34. Knickmeyer, E. (2003, April 19). Marines keep looters from $1 billion in gold. Rocket-propelled grenades fail to penetrate vaults. *Milwaukee Journal Sentinel.* Retrieved December 22, 2003, from JSOnline http://www.jsonline.com/news/gen/apr03/134505.asp[34]

35. Davidson, A. (1999). *The Oxford Companion to Food.* New York: Oxford University Press, p. 389.[35]

36. Parshall, Jonathan and Tully Anthony (2005). *Shattered Sword: The Untold Story of the Battle of Midway,* p. 210. [36]

37. Elliott, C. (2003, June). Lagging behind? Get ahead of jet lag before it gets the best of you. *Entrepreneur, 31,* 24.[37]

38. Loewen, J. W. (1995). *Lies My Teacher Told Me: Everything Your American History Textbook Got Wrong.* New York: Simon and Schuster, Inc., p. 262.[38]

39. Goleman, D. (1995). *Emotional Intelligence: Why It Can Matter More Than IQ.* New York: Bantam Books, p. 124.[39]

40. Moore, L. (2003, April). A conversation with Maya Angelou at 75. *Smithsonian,* 34, 96.[40]

41. Omang, J. (2003, May 18). Daughter of fortune. *The Washington Post,* p. T05.[41]

42. DeGeneres, Ellen (2003). *The Funny Thing Is...* New York: Simon and Schuster, p.71. [42]

43. Ambrose, S. (1996) *Undaunted courage: Meriwether Lewis, Thomas Jefferson and the Opening of the American West.* New York: Ambrose-Tubbs, Inc. p.471.[43]

44. Dixon, R. (2003, April 26). After the war environmental effects. *Los Angeles Times,* p. 11.[44]

45. Martin, J. (2003, November 31). Who doesn't want a tip? *St. Louis Post-Dispatch.* Retrieved December 22, 2003, from the St. Louis Post-Dispatch (stltoday.com) database.[45]

46. Vijayan, J. (2003, May 19). Data center security spending on the rise, surveys show security projects get funded despite tight budgets. *Computerworld, 37,* 8.[46]

47. Abrams, A. (2003, April). Depth in lights and darks: Cecile Baird creates dynamic colored-pencil and oil still lifes with a keen sense of palette and a devotion to light. *American Artist, 67,* 50-8.[47]

48. Akasie, J. (2000, February 21). Car Crazy. *Forbes. 165,* 54a.[48]

49. Dater, A. (2003, April 7). Avalanche 5, Blues 2 - Colorado clinches division title. *The Denver Post,* p.1.[49]

50. Reid, T. R. (2003, May). The Sherpas. *National Geographic,* p. 64.[50]

51. Reitman, V. (2003, March 24). Healing sound of a word: "sorry"; Doctors and hospitals are learning to disclose their mistakes. Patients often respond with lowered demands for damages. *Los Angeles Times,* Features Desk, p. 1.[51]

52. Greene, John, Robert (2004). *Betty Ford: Candor and Courage in The White House (Modern First Ladies).* University Press of Kansas: Lawrence, Kansas, p. 31.[52]

53. Fort, T. (2003, March 1). Rites of spring. *The Times*, Features, p. 3.[53]
54. Gladwell, M. (2002). *The Tipping Point: How Little Things Can Make a Big Difference.* USA: Little, Brown and Company, p. 163.[54]
55. Belsky, G. (1999). *Why Smart People Make Big Money Mistakes and How To Correct Them: Lessons From The New Science Of Behavioral Economics.* New York: Fireside, p. 98.[55]
56. McManus, E. R. (2003). *Uprising: A Revolution of the Soul.* Nashville, TN: Thomas Nelson, Inc., p. 51.[56]
57. Bryson, B. (2003). *A Short History of Nearly Everything.* New York: Random House, Inc., p. 38.[57]
58. Page, T. (2003, April 4). The NSO's strong finish at the start. *The Washington Post*, p. 8.[58]
59. Walker, C. (2003, May 26). Wreath-laying honors memory of the fallen; Iraq war lends gravity to salute to war dead. *The Baltimore Sun*, p. 2B.[59]
60. Logan, G. (2003, May 15). Rest for weary; Scott plans next round from TV chair. *Newsday*, p. A73.[60]
61. Bondy, F. (2003, March 27). Hughes on edge view from 6th another world. *Daily News*, p. 98.[61]
62. Crane, D. (2003, May 31). Soaring dollar makes Canada less competitive. *Toronto Star*, p. C02.[62]
63. Johnson, C. (2004). *The Sorrows of Empire: Militarism, Secrecy, and the End of the Republic.* New York: Henry Holt and Company, LLC, p. 49.[63]
64. Baker, K. (2001, April). Another day of infamy. *American Heritage*, *52*, 25.[64]
65. Wilson-Smith, A. (2001, August 6). The biz of journalism, and vice versa. *Maclean's*, p. 4.[65]
66. Asim, J. (2003, February 11). Tackling the riddle of race. *The Washington Post*, p. 03.[66]
67. Kurtenbach, E. (2003, November 3). General Motors to launch Cadillacs in China. *The Santa Fe New Mexican.* Retrieved December 22, 2003, from the Santa Fe New Mexico database (www.santafenewmexican.com)[67]
68. McNamara, E. (2003, May 14). Poor timing for a "prank." *The Boston Globe*, p. 1.[68]
69. Huber, P. (1998, May 18). The energy diet that flopped. *Forbes*, *161*, 306.[69]
70. Dumas, A. (1996). *The Count of Monte Cristo.* New York: Random House, Inc., p.365.[70]
71. Manley, W. (1994, April 1). You read it here first. *Booklist*, *90*, 1408.[71]
72. Yoshino, K. (2003, March 12). Orange County: Letter proves its innocence, Anaheim utility says. *Los Angeles Times*, p. 3.[72]
73. Ureneck, Lou (2007). *Backcast: Fatherhood, Fly-fishing, and a River Journey through the Heart of Alaska.* New York: St. Martins Press, p. 195.[73]
74. Stephenson, Neal (1999). *Cryptonomicon.* New York: HarperCollins, p. 399.[74]
75. Bryson, B. (2003). *A Short History of Nearly Everything.* USA: Broadway Books, p. 358.[75]
76. Cockburn, A. (2000, April), Yemen united. *National Geographic*, *197*, 30.[76]
77. Faber, M. (2002). *The Crimson Petal and the White.* Orlando, FL: Harcourt, Inc., p. 91.[77]
78. Davies, G. (2001, October 13). Celtic mixture provides intoxicating brew of emotions. *The Times* (London), Sport.[78]
79. Murphy, C. (2002, September 2). D.C. gets it almost right. *Fortune*, *146*, 38.[79]
80. Kazerooni, I. (2003, April 20). Role of ministers of faith must be as messengers for peace and hope. *The Denver Post*, p. 4.[80]
81. Boswell, T. (2002, July 22). More than a little doubt about it. *The Washington Post*, p. 1.[81]
82. Tanner, B. (2003, December 4). Single mom tries to keep her job while fighting lupus. *The Wichita Eagle*, p. 4B.[82]

83. Melley, B. (2003, November 28). Bears Used to City Living Face Greater Risks. *The Santa Fe New Mexican*. Retrieved December 22, 2003, from the Santa Fe New Mexican database (www.santafenewmexican.com).[83]
84. Hood, L. (2003, April 27). On college, "fit" a critical word. *San Antonio Express-News*, p. 8T.[84]
85. Levine, M. (2002). *A Mind at a Time*. New York: Simon and Schuster, p.174.[85]
86. Deam, J. (2003, February 10). The future of space? *The Denver Post*, p. 1.[86]
87. Stuertz, M. (2002, December 5). Green giant. Nobel laureate Norman Borlaug is credited with saving the lives of 1 billion people. So why is a small cadre of activist bent on tarnishing his legacy? *Dallas Observer*. Retrieved Dec. 17, 2003, from http://www.dallasobserver.com/issues/2002-12-05/feature.html/1/index.html[87]
88. Eliot, L. (1999) *What'sGgoing on in There? How the Brain andMmind Develop in the First Five years of Life*. New York: Bantom Books, p.55.[88]
89. Velin, B. (2003, May 19). Gervin still loves game. *USA Today*, p. 7.[89]
90. Reid, T. R. (2003, May). The Sherpas. *National Geographic*, p. 71.[90]
91. Starr, P. (2002, November). The repudiation syndrome. *The American Prospect. 13*, 2-4.[91]
92. Hicks, Esther and Hicks, Jerry (2007). *The Astonishing Power of Emotions*. USA: Hay House, p. 77.[92]
93. Saporito, B. (2001, November 19). Yer Out! Baseball says two poor teams have to go. Players wonder if the owners are just playing hardball. *Time, 158*, 149.[93]
94. A compromise from the crusader. (2000, November 13). *Business Week*, p.196.[94]
95. Levine, M. (2002). *A Mind at a Time*. New York: Simon and Schuster, p. 320.[95]
96. Forester, C. S. (1978). *Mr. Midshipman Hornblower*. USA: Little, Brown and Company, p. 118.[96]
97. Brokaw, T. (1998).*The Greatest Generation*. New York: Random House, p.68.[97]
98. The road to Marathon. (2002, October 12). *The Economist*.[98]
99. O'Sullivan, J. (2002, November 25). A rendezvous with reality: Are immigrants needed to fill our jobs and make us grow? *National Review*, 54, p. A.[99]
100. Bleau, L. (2003, June 15). Detractors digging in against land proposal. *Tampa Tribune*, p. 4.[100]
101. Picknett, L. (1997). *The Templar Revelation: Secret Guardians of the True Identity of Christ*. New York: Touchstone, p. 97.[101]
102. Reibstein, L. (1997, August 25). The "cell from hell": Pfiesteria strikes again— in the Chesapeake Bay. *Newsweek, 130*, 63.[102]
103. Peters, J. (2003, April). Remission of gin: What 18th-century London can teach us about fighting vice. *Washington Monthly, 35*, 52.[103]
104. Miller, N. (2002, March 14). The film fest that turns a planet into a star. *The Washington Post*, p. 5.[104]
105. Sherwood, K. (1992). *Chakra Therapy: For Personal Growth and Healing*. St. Paul, MN: Llewellyn Publications, p. 89.[105]
106. Bryson, B. (2003). *A Short History of Nearly Everything*. New York: Random House, p. 219.[106]
107. Austin, E. (2003, March). Giving mirth: For today's women writers, balancing work and family is agony. For Jean Kerr, it was an art form. *Washington Monthly, 35*, 43-7.[107]
108. Littler, W. (2003, February 19). On a moody snow white journey. *Toronto Star*, p. F02.[108]
109. Main, A. (2003, May 30). Jail: It's a hard cell for inside trader Rivkin. *Australian Financial Review*, p. 1.[109]
110. Hosseini, Khaled (2004). *The Kite Runner*. New York: Berkley Publishing Group, p. 10.[110]
111. Nicholas, P. (2003, May 16). Hahn, chief rip council over funding. *Los Angeles Times*, p. 3.[111]

112. Ferguson, N. (N/A). *The Rise and Demise of the British World Order and the Lessons for Global Power.* Boulder, CO: Perseus Books Group, p. 301.[112]

113. Love, S. (1997, February 24). A surgeon's challenge: We need to better than the "slash, burn and poison" approach to breast cancer. *Newsweek, 129,* 60.[113]

114. Gutmann, D. (1998, Winter). The paternal imperative. *American Scholar, 67,* 118.[114]

115. Panel seeks to curb gang activity. (2003, April 24). *The Boston Globe,* p. 2.[115]

116. Betty Crocker (Eds.) (2000). *Betty Crocker's Cookbook: Everything You Need to Know to Cook Today.* New York: Hungry Minds, Inc., p. 87.[116]

117. Briggs, C. (2003, May 16). Spiritual and sexual awakenings, a parent's decline, growing up with strangers—four women's critical life passages. *The Washington Post,* p. 13.[117]

118. Schneider, M. (2002, January 14). Disney re-learns its ABC's: New topper, sked changes may not be enough to right the ship. *Variety, 385,* 43.[118]

119. The family act. (2003, May 12). *The New Yorker, 79,* 100.[119]

120. McLaughlin, E. (2002). *The Nanny Diaries.* New York: St. Martin's Press, p. 4.[120]

121. Growe, S. J. (2003, April 5). Empowering our grandchildren is our finest task. *Toronto Star,* p. K08.[121]

122. Deford, F. (2002, December 16). Just say no: Hard-charging IOC veteran Dick Pound has a new mission—to end drug use in the Games. *Sports Illustrated, 97,* R9.[122]

123. Suiter, J. (2003, April 27). Wish they were here. *Sunday Times* (London), p. 5.[123]

124. Kunzig, R. (2002, October 7). Turning the tide. *U.S. News and World Report,* p. 66.[124]

125. Andrews, P. (2000, July 9). *The Seattle Times,* p.N3.[125]

126. Hart, J. (1990, September 17). Randall Jarrell: A literary life. *National Review, 42,* 48.[126]

127. Bart, P. (2003, January 6). The back lot. *Daily Variety, News,* p. 4.[127]

128. Cold War. (May 2000). *Harper's Magazine, 300,* 96.[128]

129. Jack Lynch (Ed.) (2004). *Samuel Johnson's Book of Insults: A Compendium of Snubs, Sneers, Slights and Effronteries from the 18th Century's Master.* New York: Walker and Co.[129]

130. Mallon, T. (2002, February). Books and Critics - Books: William Kennedy's greatest game - Roscoe has a lyricism and a gusto rarely achieved in serious American novels about politics. *The Atlantic Monthly, 289,* 93.[130]

131. Stephenson, A. (2003, January 16). Readers can walk in the shoes of Lewis and Clark. *USA Today,* p. 5D.[131]

132. Long, C. (2002). *Embellish Chic: Detailing Ready-To-Wear.* Newtown, CT: The Taunton Press, Inc., p. 3.[132]

133. O'Reilly, S. (2001, September 1). Ulrike Kubatta: Profile. *Art Review,* p. 53.[133]

134. Dumb and dumber: Does it really matter if IQ scores go up or down? (2002, March 2). *New Scientist, 173,* 3.[134]

135. Dickinson, A. (2002, March 4). Hey, you! That's mine! Dividing family heirlooms can rekindle or begin the ugliest of family feuds. Here's how some families are sorting the goods. *Time, 159,* F1.[135]

136. Henricks, M. (2001, July). Loosen up! *Entrepreneur, 29,* 97.[136]

137. Stephen E. D. & Heiman, S. (1998). *New Strategic Selling.* New York: Time Warner Books, p. 423.[137]

138. Daidoji, Y. (1999). *Code of the Samurai: A Modern Translation of the Bushido Shoshinsu.* Boston: Tuttle Publishing., p. 1.[138]

139. Danini, C. (2003, June 1). *San Antonio Express-News,* p. 6B.[139]

140. Perry, P. (1996, September-October). Safe under the sun. Saturday Evening Post, 268, 42-52.[140]

141. Perkins, S. (2003, April 5). Cannibal dinosaur known by its bones. *Science News, 163,* 211.[141]

142. Foucault, M. (1995). *Discipline and Punish: The Birth of the Prison.* New York: Random House, p. 40 (Book is quoting another source).[142]

143. Biederman, C. (2002, December 19). Long live the poison pen. There are two kinds of critics: those who criticize, and those who don't. *Dallas Observer*. Retrieved December 17, 2003, from http://www.dallasobserver.com/issues/2002-12-19/arts.html/1/index.htm[143]

144. Meyer, E. (2003, May 10). Searching out sunken ships. *The Washington Post*, p. B03.[144]

145. Tepper, A. (2002, December 2). Atop the volcano. *The Nation, 275*, 25.[145]

146. Willing, R. (2003, May 23). Attitudes ease toward medical marijuana. *USA Today*, p.3A.[146]

147. Thompson, M. (2000). *Raising Cain: Protecting the Emotional Life of Boys*. New York: The Ballantine Publishing Group, p. 244.[147]

148. Ambrose, S. (1996) *Undaunted Courage: Meriwether Lewis Thomas Jefferson and the Opening of the American West*. New York: Ambrose-Tubbs, Inc, p. 339.[148]

149. Ivins, M. (2002). *Shrub: The Short but Happy Political Life of George W. Bush*. New York: Random House, Inc., p. 142.[149]

150. Mashberg, T. (1997, September 24). Cop admits losing key evidence in Youngworth case. *The Boston Herald*, p. O16.[150]

151. Smolowe, J. (2001, October 22). First friend: Called on in a crisis, British Prime Minister Tony Blair proves a stand-up ally. *People Weekly, 56*, 147.[151]

152. Brox, J. (2002, Autumn). Dreaming of dunghills. *American Scholar, 71*, 136.[152]

153. Green, A. (2002, December 5). Snow an executive decision. Storm: When the snowflakes fall, as predicted for today, public officials had better be ready to respond—or else. *The Baltimore Sun*, p. 1B.[153]

154. Dumas père, Alexandre and Buss, Robin. (2003). *The Count of Monte Cristo*. New York: Penguin Books, p. 1075. [154]

155. Neilsen, M. (1999, June 19). Stardust memories. *America, 180*, 18.[155]

156. Katahn, M. (1986). *The Rotation Diet*. New York: W. W. Norton and Company, Inc., p. 113.[156]

157. Collier, M. (2002). *Starting an eBay Business for Dummies*. New York: Wiley Publishing, Inc., p. 215.[157]

158. Wood, J. (2003, April). Cult of the master: The later Henry James was a master of technique. But how good a novelist was he? *The Atlantic Monthly, 291*, 102-9.[158]

159. Eade, R. (2003, May 14). Here's the beef! We asked for the works—and got the best-dressed burger in town. Happy barbecue season. *Ottawa Citizen*, p. B8.[159]

160. Noden, M. (1993, April 26). Jogging and spitting. *Sports Illustrated, 78*, 28-31.[160]

161. Weissbluth, M. (1999). *Healthy Sleep Habits, Happy Child*. New York: The Ballantine Publishing Group, p. 68.[161]

162. Faber, M. (2002). *The Crimson Petal and the White*. Orlando, FL: Harcourt, Inc, p. 563.[162]

163. Butcher, Jim (2001). *Grave Peril*. New York: New American Library, p. 81. [163]

164. Cussler, Clive (2007). *The Chase by Clive*. New York: Penguin Group, p. 198. [164]

165. Deans, J. (2003, May 30). MediaGuardian: One more slip and you are for it. *The Guardian*, p. 25.[165]

166. Kidder, R. M. (1995). *How Good People Make Tough Choices: Resolving the Dilemmas of Ethical Living*. New York: Simon and Schuster, Inc., p. 118.[166]

167. Ritter, J. (2003, February 10). Celebrating home-grown chocolate. *Chicago-Sun Times*, News Special Addition, p. 5.[167]

168. Platoni, K. (2003, June). Great expectations. *Smithsonian*, p. 61.[168]

169. Dawson, V. (2003, May). Comfort zone: A cardigan Fred Rogers made every kid feel cozy and warm. *Smithsonian, 34*, 31.[169]

170. Anderson, L. (2003, May 16). Planning chief working to copy blueprint of previous job; Rutter modeling office after Howard operation; Anne Arundel. *The Baltimore Sun*, p. 1B.[170]

171. Caro, Robert (1975). *The Power Broker: Robert Moses and the Fall of New York*. New York: Random House, p. 278. [171]
172. Garrahan, M. (2002, October 1). My travel founder keeps the faith: Outgoing chairman believes business is in "good shape," says Matthew Garrahan. *Financial Times*, p. 24.[172]
173. Meadow, J. B. (2003, November 29). Do fur sales hit below the pelt? Animal-rights groups don't hide feelings on matter. *Rockymountainnews.com*. Retrieved December 23, 2003, from the Rocky Mountain News database (Rockymountainnews.com).[173]
174. Lahr, J. (2003, April 14). Lost in language. *The New Yorker, 79*, 88.[174]
175. McNulty, T. (2003, May 2). Explosive story of "Krakatoa" places eruption in history. *The Seattle Times*, p. H40.[175]
176. Rees, M. (2001). *Our Cosmic Habitat*. Princeton, NJ: Princeton University Press, p. 16.[176]
177. Hamilton, A. (2002, September 16). Look who's on the telephone! The latest videophone looks great and is easy to set up. Will it succeed where all the rest have failed? *Time, 160*, 86.[177]
178. Reform's last gasp: European takeovers. (2003, May 24). *The Economist, 367*, 65.[178]
179. Burke, M. (2003, June 9). Funny business. *Forbes, 171*, 173.[179]
180. Capuzzi Simon, C. (2002, December 24). The happy heretic: Martin Seligman thinks psychologists should help people be happy. Who could possibly have a problem with that? *The Washington Post*, p. F01.[180]
181. Jerome, R., Karlin, B., Carlin, P., Fields-Meyer, T., Foege, A., & Miller, S. (1998, September 21). From the heart. *People Weekly, 49*, 60.[181]
182. Bryson, B. (2003). *A Short History of Nearly Everything*. USA: Broadway Books, p. 358.[182]
183. Alexander, C. (1977). *A Pattern Language: Towns, Buildings, Construction*. United States: Christopher Alexander, p. 356.[183]
184. Andrews. A. (2002). *The Traveler's Gift: Seven Decisions that Determine Personal Success*. Nashville, TN: Thomas Nelson, Inc., p. 136.[184]
185. Bennett, B. (2002, February 11). Get away to Taipei: Weekend wanderings. *Time International, 159*, 6.[185]
186. Weiner, Eric (2008). *The Geography of Bliss: One Grump's Search for the Happiest Places in the World*. New York: Hachette Book Group, p. 12. [186]
187. Hartman, T. (2003, July 10). Dividing the waters. A fight over an irrigation ditch pits Rocky Ford's rural way of life against the thirst of a growing Aurora. *Rockymountainnews.com*. Retrieved December 23, 2003, from the *Rocky Mountain News* database.[187]
188. KIdder, David S. and Oppenheim, Noah D. (2007). *The Intellectual Devotional: American History: Revive Your Mind, Complete Your Education, and Converse Confidently about Our Nation's Past*. New York: Rodale Books, p. 24. [188]
189. Dess, N. (2001, July). The new body-mind connection. *Psychology Today, 34*, 30.[189]
190. Budick, A. (2003, April 19). Fashion show chronicles women's political liberation. *The Seattle Times*, p. E4.[190]
191. Strauss, G. (2003, January 13). Birkenstock sticks toe in future with an eye to past. *USA Today*, p. 1B.[191]
192. Burton, Katherine (2007). *Hedge Hunters: Hedge Fund Masters on the Rewards, the Risk, and the Reckoning*. New York: Bloomberg Press, front cover. [192]
193. Groer, A. (2002, June 13). Political papers. *The Washington Post*, p. H01.[193]
194. Shprintz, J. (1999, June 14). DreamWorks avoids mouse hunt for info. *Variety, 375*, 2.[194]
195. McCall, K. (2003, June). In their corner: Focus your coaching efforts where they'll pack the most punch—on your top performers. *Entrepreneur, 31*, 79-81.[195]
196. Lowry. R. (2003, May 21). No reason to extend meaningless ban on assault weapons. *The Atlanta Journal-Constitution*, p. 19A.[196]

197. Briggs, B. (2003, February 13). International socialite whose charm opens doors of the rich and famous. *The Herald*, p. 3.[197]

198. Ambrose, S. (1996). *Undaunted Courage: Meriwether Lewis Thomas Jefferson and the Opening of the American West*. New York: Touchstone, p. 392.[198]

199. Wilson-Smith, A. (2003, April 21). The Media, unbound: There's a theory that true objectivity is impossible. So should we even try? *Maclean's*, p.4.[199]

200. Wellman, L. (2003, January 22). In the councils of war, nothing's cast in concrete. *The San Francisco Chronicle*, p. D10.[200]

201. Buckingham, M. (2001). *Now, Discover Your Strengths*. New York: The Free Press, p. 19.[201]

202. Glickman, R. (2002). *Optimal Thinking: How to Be Your Best Self*. New York: John Wiley and Sons, Inc., p. 178.[202]

203. Morton, A. (1998). *Diana: Her True Story in Her Own Words*. New York: Simon and Schuster, Inc., p. 256.[203]

204. Gaither, C. (2003, May 19). Technology & innovation: Mass. Bill aimed at blocking spam measure would mandate warnings. *The Boston Globe*, p. C1.[204]

205. Moser, B. (2002, January 28). For whom the pots clang. *Newsweek International*, p. 29.[205]

206. Baker, K. (2001, July). Funny business. *American Heritage*, *52*, 20.[206]

207. Hamm, S. (1994, April 4). The odd man out. *PC Week*, *11*, A1-3.[207]

208. Ratto, R. (2003, May 25). Cure for road-weary club may be in the dirt. *The San Francisco Chronicle*, p. B1.[208]

209. Friedman, M. (1980). *Free to Choose: A Personal Statement*. Orlando, FL: Harcourt, Inc., p. 144.[209]

210. Perdue, L. (2000). *Daughter of God*. New York: Tom Doherty Associates, LLC., p. 145.[210]

211. Risk of injury comes into play. Young athletes should not ignore preventive measures and exams. (2003, October 28). *Rockymountainnews.com*. Retrieved December 23, 2003, from the *Rocky mountain News* database (www.rockymountainnews.com).[211]

212. Keen, J. (2003, May 29). President's journey full of diplomatic challenges Europe, Mideast relations on line. *USA Today*, p. 6A.[212]

213. Vesilind, P. (1997, January). Sri Lanka. *National Geographic, 191*, p. 110.[213]

214. Nylund, E. (2003). First Strike (Halo). New York: The Random House Publishing Group, p. 122.[214]

215. Milton, G. (2003). *Samurai William: The Englishman Who Opened the East*. New York: Farrar, Straus and Guoux, p. 306.[215]

216. Back to square one. (2003, March 8). *The Times*, Features, p. 25.[216]

217. Calm in a cyclone: Profile of a leader. (2002, April 1). *Business Week*, p. 88.[217]

218. A risky "privilege" despite industry claims, economic facts about casinos are not reassuring. (2003, February 9). *Omaha World Herald*, p. 10B.[218]

219. Witcover, J. (2003, May 14). McGovern: I am not an isolationist. *The Baltimore Sun*, p.13A.[219]

220. Corfield, P. (1997, December). Laughing at the learned. *History Today, 47*, 3-6.[220]

221. Noonan, C. (2001, March). Exhibiting online. *American Artist, 65*, 58.[221]

222. Vital Signs: After nine seasons of fake blood, real love and backstage pranks, ER celebrates its 200th episode with infectious enthusiasm and a behind-the-scenes baby boom. (2003, May 12) *People Weekly, 59*, 184.[222]

223. Martins, G. (2003, May 11). Soccer: Revs even score, defeat Galaxy to avenge cup loss. *The Boston Herald*, p. B10.[223]

224. Townsend, K. (2003, Spring). Starting to ride at sixty-five. *American Scholar, 72*, 79.[224]

225. Chabon, M. (2000). *The Amazing Adventures of Kavalier and Clay*. New York: Picador, p. 125.[225]

226. Neff, C. (1983, February 7). Billy cracks the vault. *Sports Illustrated, 58*, 30.[226]

227. Arouet Voltaire, F. (1947). *Candide*. Toronto, Ontario: Penguin Books, p. 7.[227]

228. Botto, L. (2002). *At This Theatre.* New York: Applause Theater and Cinema Books, p. 244.[228]
229. Larson, E. (2003). *The Devil in the White City: Murder, Magic, and Madness at the Fair That Changed America.* New York: Crown Publishers, p. 287.[229]
230. Formichelli, L. (2002, January-February). Big disasters result in tiny babies. *Psychology Today*, 35, 21.[230]
231. Goleman, D. (1997) *Emotional Intelligence: Why It Can Matter More Than IQ.* New York: Bantam Books, p. 231.[231]
232. Mortenson, Greg and Oliver, Relin David (2007). *Three Cups of Tea: One Man's Mission to Promote Peace.* New York: Penguin Books, p. 138. [232]
233. Douglas, K. (2002, November 2). Humans with altitude: Some are born to the high life, others have it thrust upon them. Kate Douglas discovers how people survive on thin air. *New Scientist*, p. 36-40.[233]
234. Bradley, J. (2000). *Flags of Our Fathers.* New York: Bantam Books, p. 62.[234]
235. Jeffrey, D. (1996, March 30). Wall Street credibility: Taking stock of dwindling investments, analysts say music retailers must make some tough decisions to turn things around. *Billboard, 108*, 68.[235]
236. Weissbluth, M. (1999). *Healthy Sleep Habits, Happy Child.* New York: The Ballantine Publishing Group, p. 243.[236]
237. Turner, A. (2003, May 18). In her element; Woman uses love of meteorology to help public weather storms. *The Houston Chronicle*, p. A-36.[237]
238. Webster, D. (2000, November). Goes to hell. *National Geographic, 198*, 50.[238]
239. Kidd, S. M. (2002). *The Secret Life of Bees.* New York: Penguin Putnam, Inc., p. 277.[239]
240. Jackson Jr., H. (2003, June 2). After losing 50 pounds, he can join family activities again. *St. Louis Post-Dispatch*, p. 4.[240]
241. Shmith, M. (2003, June 1). Thanks for the mnemonics. *Sunday Age*, p. 16.[241]
242. Ignelzi, R. J. (2002, July 4). Techniques can help sharpen the mind. *The San Diego Union-Tribune*, p. E-1.[242]
243. Fitzgerald, R. (1974). *The Iliad.* USA: Anchor Books, p. 207.[243]
244. Paine, Thomas and Hook, Sidney (2003). *Common Sense, The Rights of Man and Other Essential Writings of Thomas Paine.* New York: Signet Classic, p. 364. [244]
245. Demille, N. (1985). *Word of Honor.* New York: Warner Books, Inc., p. 20.[245]
246. Picard, R. (1998). *Affective Computing.* Cambridge: MIT Press.[246]
247. Campos, C. (2003, March 17). Records' secrecy sought; Legislators fear criminals might use the documents. *The Atlanta Journal and Constitution*, p. 3B.[247]
248. Hill, J. (2003, May 29). Electronic games. *The Age, Green Guide*, Livewire, p. 16.[248]
249. Anderson, D. (2002, June 29). A class above the kinda dirty. *Sydney Morning Herald*, p. 11.[249]
250. Striking decision. (1994, September 5). *People Weekly*, 42, 54.[250]
251. Kulman, L., Firor, N. & Boser U. (2001, February 26). Job jitters? Stay calm. Hiring still outstrips firing. *U. S. News and World Report, 130*, 56.[251]
252. *The World Almanac and Book of Facts 2004.* (2004). New York: World Almanac Books, p. 179.[252]
253. Spinks, P. (1991, November 2). The making of the new environmental consciousness. *New Scientist, 132*, 46.[253]
254. Manoyan, D. (2003, May 9). Sign of the Times: Male coaches feel unwanted in women's basketball. *Milwaukee Journal Sentinel*, p. 01C.[254]
255. Loewen, J. W. (1995). *Lies My Teacher Told Me: Everything Your American History Textbook Got Wrong.* New York: Touchstone, p. 283.[255]
256. Ross, Alex (2007). *The Rest Is Noise: Listening to the Twentieth Century.* New York: Farrar, Straus and Giroux, p. 333. [256]
257. Spiros, D. (2003, May 12). Looking for a weakness; Riddling him with shots was not the answer. But Wild players insist that Anaheim goalie Jean-Sebastien Giguere can be solved. *Star Tribune*, p. 4S.[257]

258. Roessing, W. (1988, April). The madcap side of pro golf. *Saturday Evening Post, 260*, 48.[258]
259. Baldwin, T. & Bennett, R. (2002, November 16). Ministers seek more control of firefighters. *The Times, Home News*, 14.[259]
260. Finlay, V. (2002). *Color: A Natural History of the Palette*. New York: The Ballantine Publishing Group, p. 50.[260]
261. Bronson, P. (2002). *What Should I Do with My Life?* New York: Random House, p. 139.[261]
262. DiManno, R. (2003, April 21). Hunt for the disappeared leads to hellish tunnels. *Toronto Star*, p. A02.[262]
263. Peers, E. A. (1990). *Dark Night of the Soul*. New York: Doubleday, p. 41.[263]
264. McPherson, James M. (2003). *Battle Cry of Freedom: The Civil War Era (Oxford History of the United States)*. Oxford University Press, p. 455. [264]
265. Edwards, M. (1996, December), Lord of the Mongols: Genghis. *National Geographic*, 190, 4-38.[265]
266. Mistry, Rohinton (1995). *A Fine Balance*. New York: Vintage Books, back cover. [266]
267. Yamey, G. (2001, May 19). Global campaign to eradicate malaria: Roll Back Malaria has achieved a high profile but little real action. *British Medical Journal, 322*, 1191.[267]
268. Breathnach, S. B. (1995). *Simple Abundance: A Daybook of Comfort and Joy*. New York: Warner Books, Inc., p. 31.[268]
269. Kennedy, K. (1999, November 9). Inside the NHL. *Sports Illustrated, 91*, 160.[269]
270. Petroski, H. (1992). *To Engineer Is Human: The Role of Failure in Successful Design*. New York: *Vintage Books*, p. 177.[270]
271. Williams, P. (2003, April 14). Codes of etiquette. *The Nation, 276*, 10.[271]
272. Schultz, Patricia (2007). *1,000 Places to See in the U.S.A. & Canada Before You Die*. New York: Workman Publishing, p. 436. [272]
273. Carnegie, D. (1981). *How to Win Friends and Influence People*. New York: Simon and Schuster, Inc., p. 82.[273]
274. Nelson, S. (2003, May 17). State looks at deregulating auto rates ideas for change solicited from task force, others. *The Boston Globe*, p. C1.[274]
275. Bryson, B. (2003). *A Short History of Nearly Everything*. New York: Random House, Inc., p. 111.[275]
276. McInnis, S. (2003, May 21). Is legislation the answer to forest mismanagement? Yes: Bill gets rid of dangerous red tape. *The Denver Post*, p. B-07.[276]
277. Martel, Y. (2001). *Life of Pi*. Orlando, FL: Harcourt, Inc., p. 69.[277]
278. Sisson, D. (1984, September). Did the Irish discover America? *Saturday Evening Post, 256*, 52.[278]
279. Park, E. (1991, January). Around the mall and beyond. *Smithsonian, 21*, 22-5.[279]
280. Peck, M. S. (1978). *The Road Less Traveled, 25th Anniversary Edition: A New Psychology of Love, Traditional Values and Spiritual Growth*. New York: Touchstone, p. 24.[280]
281. Lemonick, M. (2003, March 31). Feb. 28, 1953, Eureka: The double helix. *Time, 161*, A30.[281]
282. Levine, M. (2002). *A Mind at a Time*. New York: Simon and Schuster, p. 286.[282]
283. Peru:HowFujimoriletreformfallflat. (2000, February). *Business Week*, p. 25.[283]
284. Intindola, B. (2003, March 16). Buffettlaysmoreheatonboards. *The Houston Chronicle*, Business. p. 8.[284]
285. Loewen, J. W. (1995) Lies My Teacher Told Me. Everything Your American History Textbook Got Wrong. New York: Touchstone, p. 38, [285]
286. Bryson B. (2003). A Short History of Nearly Everything. Broadway Books, p. 217.[286]
287. Bambarger, B. (2000, May 20). Classicalkeepingscore. *Billboard*, 112, 66.[287]
288. Ackerman, Diane (2007). *The Zookeeper's Wife: A War Story*. W. W. New York: Norton and Company, p. 141. [288]

289. Goleman, D. (1998). *Working with Emotional Intelligence*. New York: Bantam Books, p. 184.[289]

290. Springer, S. (2003, March 20). Celticsnotebook:They'remisfiringfromlongrange. *The Boston Globe*, p. F5. [290]

291. Foundas, S. (2003, May 5). I Witness. *Variety*, 390, 37.[291]

292. Adams, D. (2002). The Ultimate Hitchhiker's Guide to the Galaxy. *USA: Ballantine Publishing Group*, p. 8.[292]

293. (2002, April 14). Down to the tax wire. *San Francisco Chronicle*, p. G3.[293]

294. Morgenstern, J. (1998). *Organizing from the Inside Out*. New York: Henry Hold and Company, LLC., p. 31.[294]

295. Levy, C. (2003, May 1). Frankie Hewitt dies at 71; Led revival of Ford's Theatre. *The Washington Post*, p. B06.[295]

296. Cavendish, R. (2002, February). Birth of Victor Hugo February 26th, 1802. *History Today*, 52, 55.[296]

297. Collins, A. (2003). *The Draconomicon (Dungeons and Dragons)*. Renton, WA: Wizards of the Coast, Inc., p. 267.[297]

298. McCarthy, T. J. (2002, October 14). How will I be remembered? *America*, p. 6.[298]

299. Sokol, M. (2003, June 6). The fine art of opening a business in Keystone. *St. Petersburg Times*, p. 1.[299]

300. Senge, P. M. (1990). *The Fifth Discipline*. New York: Doubleday, p. 19.[300]

301. Bradbury, E. (2000, September). Europe's institutionalized corruption. *Contemporary Review*, 277, 177.[301]

302. Pomiewozic, J. (2001, October 15). Through a different lens. *Time*, 158, 94.[302]

303. Covey, S. R. (1989). *Seven Habits of Highly Effective People*. New York: Fireside, p. 209.[303]

304. Koeppel, F. (2003, March 16). The wizard of artistic enigma - Barney concocts an exotic potion and labels it "the cremaster cycle." *The Commercial Appeal*, p. F1.[304]

305. Goldsmith, J. (2002, December 23). It's buyout beware for biz. *Variety*, 389, 4.[305]

306. O'Connor, A. (2003, May 19). On the trail of tainted art; an historian is in increasing demand to establish the ownership of valuable works stolen during the Holocaust. *Los Angeles Times*, p. 2.[306]

307. Magazine poll ranks city 13th as an arts destination. (2003, June 3). *Pittsburgh Post-Gazette*, p. B-2.[307]

308. Pink, Daniel H. (2006). *A Whole New Mind: Why Right-Brainers Will Rule the Future*. New York: The Berkley Publishing Group, p. 57. [308]

309. Selvin, J. (2002, July 14). Critic raised the bar. *The San Francisco Chronicle*, p. 54.[309]

310. Chevalier, T. (1999). *Girl with a Pearl Earring*. New York: Penguin Group, p. 174.[310]

311. Davis, W. (1999, August). Vanishing cultures. *National Geographic*, 196, p. 62.[311]

312. Leigh, R. (1983). *Holy Blood, Holy Grail*. New York: Dell Publishing, p. 36.[312]

313. Patoski, J. (2003, May). Texas trails: How do you get to the heart of a state as big as a nation? It's easy—if you pick the right road. *American Heritage*, 54, S2-23.[313]

314. Jones, C. (2003, May 26). Hot carnival warms up cool mission streets; Annual parade showcases a kaleidoscope of culture. *The San Francisco Chronicle*, p. A11.[314]

315. Beck, M. (2003, July). Ready...aim...oh, well. *Oprah Magazine*, p. 63.[315]

316. Robert III, H. M. (2000). *Robert's Rules of Order*. Cambridge, MA: Perseus Books Group, p. 564.[316]

317. Homegrown help. (1998, July 6). *People Weekly*, 49, 12.[317]

318. Moffat, S. (1996, September 30). Hong Kong Jockey Club. *Fortune*, 134, 73.[318]

319. Glickman, R. (2002). *Optimal Thinking: How to Be Your Best Self*. New York: John Wiley and Sons, Inc., p.21.[319]

320. Shafer, H. (1994, November). Painting on the waterfront. *American Artist*, 58, 30.[320]

321. Woodson, J. (2003, May 20). Triple-Murderer gets death; Alfred Flores, who killed teens for refusing to join his gang, laughs at the survivors. *Los Angeles Times*, p. 1.[321]

322. Martel, Y. (2001). *Life of Pi*. Orlando, FL: Harcourt, Inc., p. 285.[322]

323. Wood, C. (2000, February). The Web is a hacker's playground. *PC World*, 18, 33.[323]

324. Brown, S. (1991). *Breath of Scandal*. New York: Warner Books, Inc., p. 148.[324]
325. Mitchell, K. (2003, February 19). "Hoarders" take animal obsession to rancid level. *The Denver Post*, p. A-01.[325]
326. Montefiore, S. S. (1993, January-February). The thrill of the kill: Inside the mind of a Russian hit man. *Psychology Today, 26*, 42.[326]
327. Martel, Y. (2001). *Life of Pi*. Orlando, FL: Harcourt, Inc., p. 212.[327]
328. Rosenthal, A. (2003, February 10). Bloody, brutal and grimly moral: Amy Rosenthal enjoys a thrillingly contemporary revenge tragedy. *New Statesman, 132*, 46.[328]
329. Manoyan, D. (2002, October 4). Burris plans to do his part; Former Packer hopes to hurt Sherman and Co. *Milwaukee Journal Sentinel*, p. 05C.[329]
330. Brinkley, D. (2003, March 31). July 20, 1969: "One Giant Leap for Mankind." *Time, 161*, A52.[330]
331. Cochrane, J. & Kola, K. (2002, December 9). The parent killer. *Newsweek International*, p. 25.[331]
332. Lansing, A. (1959). *Endurance: Shackleton's Incredible Voyage*. New York: Carroll and Graf Publishers, p. 4.[332]
333. Buckingham, M. (1999). *First, Break All the Rules: What the World's Greatest Managers Do Differently.* New York, NY: Simon and Schuster, p. Appendix E.[333]
334. Corcoran, E. (2000, October 2). Go forth and publish. *Forbes, 166*, 170.[334]
335. Hustak, A. (2003, April 12). Churchman with the soul of a financier. *The Gazette*, p. E5.[335]
336. Poitier, Sidney (2007). *The Measure of a Man: A Spiritual Autobiography*. New York: HarperCollins, p. 66. [336]
337. Hallowell, E. M. (1994). *Driven To Distraction: Recognizing and Coping withAttention Deficit Disorder from Childhood through Adulthood*. New York: Touchstone, p. 53.[337]
338. Dvorak, J. (2000, December 25). State of the banner. *Forbes, 166*, 273.[338]
339. Stipp, D. (2003, May 26). Biotech's Billion Dollar Breakthrough: A technology called RNAi has opened the door to major new drugs. Already it's revolutionizing gene research. *Fortune, 147*, 96.[339]
340. Schwartz, J. (2003, June 1). San Marcos plans to honor jazz great, native son Durham. *The Houston Chronicle*, p. 38-A.[340]
341. Maguire, Gregory (2000). *Confessions of an Ugly Stepsister.* New York: HarperCollins, p. 182. [341]
342. Saramago, J. (1995). *Blindness*. Orlando, FL: Harcourt, Inc, p. 101-102.[342]
343. Schindehette, S. & Dodd, J. (2002, June 24). The baby tamer: Dr. Harvey Karp claims he can calm almost any crying newborn—and you can too. *People Weekly, 57*, 149.[343]
344. Aubin, B. (2002, July 22). At the crossroads: How long can the country keep up its balancing act? *Maclean's*, p. 28.[344]
345. Welsh, A. M. (2003, April 14). The Lamb's spirit is willing but the sitcom script is weak. *The San Diego Union-Tribune*, p. D-3.[345]
346. Laarson, M. (2001, June 18). Starcom. *Mediaweek, 11*, SR10.[346]
347. Clark, R. (2003, April 3). The hills are alive with the sound of moaning. *The Times* (London), p. 20.[347]
348. Stayton, R. (1992, February). Hellraiser. *American Theatre, 8*, 26.[348]
349. Redding, S. (1980). *Catch Me If You Can: The True Story of a Real Fake*. Grosset and Dunlap, p. 25.[349]
350. Henricks, M. (2000, April). Change of face. *Entrepreneur, 28*, 125.[350]
351. Bryson, B. (1999). *I'm a Stranger Here Myself: Notes on Returning to America after 20 Years Away*. New York: Broadway Books, p. 215.[351]
352. Johnson, W. & Lilley, J. (1992, August 10). Swimmers for sale. *Sports Illustrated, 77*, 46.[352]
353. Coile, Z. (2003, May 22). Environmentalists worry as EPA chief steps down; Some fear successor will side with industry against pollution limits. *The San Francisco Chronicle*, p. A1.[353]

354. Hallowell, E. M. (1994). *Driven To Distraction: Recognizing and Coping with Attention Deficit Disorder from Childhood through Adulthood.* New York: Touchstone, p. 128.[354]
355. Kurcinka, M. S. (1991). *Raising Your Spirited Child: A Guide for Parents WhoseChild Is More Intense, Sensitive, Perceptive, Persistent, Energetic.* New York: HarperCollins Publishers, Inc., p. 129.[355]
356. Maister, D. (2000). *The Trusted Advisor.* New York: Simon and Schuster, p. 117.[356]
357. Csikszentmihalyi, M. (1996, July-August). The creative personality. *Psychology Today, 29,* 36.[357]
358. Friend, T. (2002, April 8). The moviegoer: Peter Bogdanovich returns to filmmaking. *The New Yorker, 78,* 36.[358]
359. Lencioni, P. M. (2002). *The Five Dysfunctions of a Team: A Leadership Fable.* New York: Jossey-Bass, p. 64.[359]
360. Shatz, A. (2002, March 24). Music: A jazz diva who's losing interest in jazz. *New York Times,* p. 1.[360]
361. Cole, R. (2003, January 8). Defence wares boost Cobham. *The Times* (London), p. 22.[361]
362. Watkins, T. H. (1999, May). The bird did its part: During the Great Depression, the blue eagle was a symbol of the National Recovery Administration. *Smithsonian, 29,* 30.[362]
363. Crow, C. (2001, March). Artists in the London landscape. *History Today, 51,* 4.[363]
364. Neill, M. (1997, November 17). Buried treasure: With attorney Roger Richman defending their rights, dead celebrities are treated like royalty. *People Weekly, 48,* 201-3.[364]
365. Borger, G. (2002, July 8). Why hate Martha? *U. S. News and World Report,* p. 17.[365]
366. Ghosh, A. (2003, May 5). Forever a prisoner. *Time, 161,* 42.[366]
367. Siegfried, D. (2002, November 1). Witt, James Lee and Morgan, James. Stronger in the broken places: Nine lessons for turning crisis into triumph. *Booklist, 99,* 463.[367]
368. Stuller, J. (1984, October). Lee Iacocca and an America that's back on its feet. *Saturday Evening Post, 256,* 46-51.[368]
369. Globe West Extra/News in brief; Union, hospital reaches tentative deal. (2003, March 24). *The Boston Globe,* p. B2.[369]
370. Shmuckler, E. (1994, March 21). Kids upfront goes down. *Mediaweek, 4,* 5.[370]
371. Padilla, D. (2003, May 14). Feisty Manuel sticks up for Thomas. *Chicago Sun-Times,* p. 145.[371]
372. Barlow, J. P. (2002, October 7). Why spy? *Forbes, ASAP, 170,* 42.[372]
373. Lord, L. (2003, January 20). A winter that "chilled like the world's end." *U. S. News and World Report,* p. 12.[373]
374. Dolgun, A. (1975) *Alexander Dolgun's Story.* New York: Alfred A. Knopf, Inc., p. 326.[374]
375. Cameron, B. (2003, May-June). Austerity blues. *American Theatre, 20,* 4.[375]
376. Done, K. (2003, May 23). Extra runway "vital for economy" says BA. *Financial Times* (London), p. 3.[376]
377. Chevalier, T. (1999). *Girl with a Pearl Earring.* New York: Penguin Books, p. 49.[377]
378. Gardner, J. (1990, December 17). Venetian palaces. *National Review, 42,* 49.[378]
379. Neal, V. (2000, April). The fall guys. *Entrepreneur, 28,* 26.[379]
380. Wiegand, D. (2003, May 23). HBO constructs a magnificent, richly detailed "House": Maggie Smith steals show in subtle role. *The San Francisco Chronicle,* p. D2.[380]
381. Covey, S. R. (1994). *First Things First: To Live, to Love, to Learn, to Leave a Legacy.* New York: Simon and Schuster, Inc., p. 104.[381]
382. Murphy, J. (2000). *The Power of Your Subconscious Mind* (Rev. Ed.). New York: Bantam Books, p.177.[382]
383. Gottman, J. M. (1999). *The Seven Principles for Making Marriage Work: A Practical Guide from the Country's Foremost Relationship Expert.* New York: Three Rivers Press, p. 9.[383]
384. A critical eye. (2001, March). *American Artist, 65,* 8.[384]

385. Kabat-Zinn, J. (1990). *Full Catastrophe Living: Using the Wisdom of Your Body and Mind to Face Stress, Pain, and Illness*. New York: Dell Publishing, p. 36.[385]
386. Elliott, D. (2002, April 29). In search of lasting heroes: With the economy in turmoil, many Asians are focused on money, not morals, writes Dorinda Elliott. But idealism is not dead, just deferred. *Time International, 159*, 58.[386]
387. Maxwell, J. C. (1999). *The 21 Indispensable Qualities of a Leader: Becoming the Person Others Will Want to Follow*. Nashville, TN: Thomas Nelson, Inc., p. 2.[387]
388. Chadiha, J. (2001, January 15). Safety valve: Following the lead of Robert Griffith, the Vikings' defense came to life and overwhelmed the Saints. *Sports Illustrated, 94*, 42.[388]
389. Bryson, B. (2003). *A Short History of Nearly Everything*. USA: Broadway Books, p. 230.[389]
390. Murphy, P. A. (1998, March-April). Ditching the years of living dangerously. *Psychology Today, 31*, 18.[390]
391. Global briefing. (2001, October 9). *Time, 158*, B7.[391]
392. Leshko, A. (2002, August). Just a snapshot? *Smithsonian*, p. 19.[392]
393. Botkin, S. C. (2003). *Lower Your Taxes - Big Time! Wealth-Building, Tax Reduction Secrets from an IRS Insider*. New York: McGraw Hill, p. 105.[393]
394. Slavin, P. (1996, May). The information age and the civil society: An interview with Jeremy Rifkin. *Phi Delta Kappan, 77*, 607.[394]
395. Rushin, S. (1997, March 3). Inside the moat. *Sports Illustrated, 86*, 68.[395]
396. Saving the forest for the trees. (2000, November 20). *Business Week*, p. 62.[396]
397. Bliss, M. (2001, October 1). The epic (cont'd): The second season of Canada's national history is just as good as the first. In fact, better. *Time International, 158*, 92.[397]
398. Walker, B. (1987, January). Tales of sunken gold and hunters of the depths. *Smithsonian, 17*, 96.[398]
399. Jenkins, B. (2003, May 9). Beane, Howe now dwelling at opposite ends of spectrum. *The San Francisco Chronicle*, p. C1.[399]
400. Vogelstein, F, Rae-Dupree, J., Sloan, P., and Holstein, W. (2000, May 1). Easy dot com, easy dot go. *U. S. News and World Report, 128*, 42.[400]

Bibliography

Atkinson, R. C. (1975). Mnemotechnics in second-language learning. *American Psychologist, 30,* 821-828.

Avila, E. & Sadoski, M. (1996). Exploring new applications of the keyword method to acquire English vocabulary. *Language Learning, 46,* 379-395.

Carney, R. N. & Levin, J. R. (1998). Coming to term with the keyword method in Introductory Psychology: A "neuromnemonic" example. *Teaching of Psychology, 25,* 132-134.

Harper Collins Webster's Dictionary. (2003). New York: Harper Collins Publishers.

Jones, M. J., Levin, M. E., Levin, J.R. & Beitzel, B.D. (2000). Can vocabulary-learning strategies and pair-learning formats be profitably combined? *Journal of Educational Psychology, 92,* 256-262.

Levin, J. R. (1982). Pictures as prose learning devices. In A. Flammer & W. Kintsch (ed.). *Discourse Processing-Advances in Psychology.* New York: North-Holland Publishing Company. p. 412-444.

Levin, J. R. (1986). Four cognitive principles of learning-strategy instruction. *Educational Psychologist, 21,* 3-17.

Levin, J. R. (1983). Pictorial strategies for school learning:Practical illustrations. In M. Pressley & J.R. Levin (Eds.), *Cognitive strategy research: Educational applications* (pp. 213-237). New York: Springer-Verlag.

Levin, J.R. (1981). The Mnemonic'80s: Keywords in the classroom. *Educational Psychologist, 16,* 65-82.

Lysynchuk, L. & Pressley, M. (1990). Vocabulary (ch.4) in *Cognitive strategy instruction that really improves children's academic performance.* Cabridge, MA: Brookline Books.

Mastropieri, M. A. & Scruggs, T. E. (1991). *Teaching students ways to remember.* BrooklineBooks: Cambridge, MA.

Merriam Webster's online dictionary. Retrieved from www.merriamwebster.com.

Procter, P. (Ed.). (1995). *Cambridge International Dictionary of English. Cambridge.* United Kingdom: Cambridge University Press.

Sternberg, R. J. (1986) Beyond IQ: *A triarchic theory of Human inteligence.* Yale University Press: New Haven, CT.

The American Heritage Dictionary. (2001). Boston, NY: Houghton Mifflin Company.

Wang, A. Y. & Thomas, H. T. (1995). Effect of keywords on long-term retention: Help or hindrance? *Journal of Educational Psychology, 87,* 468-475.

Answer Key

Review Answers

Section 1

Crossword Puzzle
Across: 5-Abhor 8-Abeyance 9-Anomaly 10-Bane 12-Assiduous 14-Attribution 15-Apocryphal 17-Attenuation

Down: 1-Alacrity 2-Ambivalence 3-Bellicose 4-Alienate 5-Audacious 6-Adulation 7-Arduous 8-Abstract 11-Aver 12-Amorphous 13-Abrogate 16-Apathy

Multiple Choice
1-b. alienated 2-d. assiduous 3-a. abstract 4-d. amorphous 5-c. abhor 6-a. abrogatcd 7-d. adulation 8-b. alacrity 9-a. averred 10-c. attribution 11-a. bellicose 12-a. abeyance 13-b. anomaly 4-c. apocryphal 15-c. arduous 16-d. audacious 17-a. bane 18-d. apathy 19-d. ambivalence 20-a. attenuated

Matching
1-E 2-R 3-C 4-J 5-M 6-K 7-T 8-A 9-H 10-L 11-N 12-P 13-D 14-O 15-F 16-G 17-I 18-Q 19-S 20-B

Section 2

Crossword Puzzle
Across: 1-Breach 3-Candor 4-Conspicuous 7-Coalesce 9-Corroborate 10-Cacophony 11-Concise 15-Burnish 17-Contumacious 18-Bequeath

Down: 2-Conciliatory 5-Castigate 6-Cognizant 7-Cursory 8-Craven 9-Capricious 12-Credulous 13-Cryptic 14-Complacent 16-Bemuse

Multiple Choice
1-b. cryptic 2-d. burnish 3-d. bequeath 4-a. cursory 5-b. cacophony 6-d. candor 7-a. capricious 8-b. contumacious 9-d. castigated 10-a. coalesced 11-b. complacent 12-b. conciliatory 13-b. concise 14-d. bemused 15-c. conspicuous 16-c. corroborated 17-a. craven 18-c. credulous 19-c. breached 20-b. cognizant

Matching
1-O 2-Q 3-H 4-R 5-G 6-S 7-K 8-I 9-E 10-J 11-P 12-B 13-D 14-T 15-L 16-F 17-A 18-C 19-M 20-N

Section 3

Crossword Puzzle
Across: 3-Disparage 5-Deter 6-Diminution 7-Dulcet
8-Devious 14-Desecrate 16-Debilitate 17-Denunciation
Down: 1-Dogmatic 2-Denigration 3-Dismantle 4-Discursive
6-Deflate 8-Disperse 9-Deleterious 10-Derision 11-Demeanor
12-Didactic 13-Debunk 15-Disdain

Multiple Choice
1-c. dulcet 2-c. denigration 3-b. debunk 4-a. deleterious
5-b. denunciation 6-a. derision 7-b. desecrated 8-a. didactic
9-a. debilitated 10-d. devious 11-c. demeanor 12-c. deter
13-a. dismantled 14-c. dogmatic 15-c. diminution
16-a. discursive 17-b. dispersed 18-b. disdain 19-d. deflate
20-a. disparaged

Matching
1-C 2-M 3-F 4-P 5-O 6-T 7-I 8-B 9-R 10-A 11-E 12-S
13-K 14-G 15-L 16-N 17-D 18-J 19-H 20-Q

Section 4

Crossword Puzzle
Across: 1-Epitome 3-Efface 4-Equivocal 8-Ebb 9-Euphoric
10-Exculpate 12-Fatuous 14-Engender 16-Extenuate 17-Evince
Down: 1-Effluvia 2-Extol 4-Empirical 5-Esoteric 6-Duplicity
7-Embellish 11-Effrontery 13-Extraneous 14-Expedient
15-Ephemeral

Multiple Choice
1-d. epitome 2-a. euphoric 3-d. duplicity 4-a. extolled
5-a. effrontery 6-d. embellished 7-b. engender 8-c. fatuous
9-c. extenuating 10-a. ephemeral 11-c. equivocal 12-b. esoteric
13-b. evinced 14-d. exculpated 15-b. effluvia 16-d. expedient
17-c. empirical 18-d. ebbed 19-b. extraneous 20-c. efface

Matching Review
1-H 2-A 3-J 4-T 5-C 6-D 7-F 8-O 9-G 10-Q 11-M 12-S
13-P 14-I 15-N 16-E 17-K 18-L 19-B 20-R

Chapter 5

Crossword Puzzle
Across: 1-Florid 5-Fitful 7-Heretic 9-Galvanize 12-Impeach
16-Iconoclast 17-Impetuous 18-Hierarchy
Down: 1-Flout 2-Gullible 3-Forlorn 4-Furtive 6-Fulsome
8-Gregarious 10-Imperative 11-Frenetic 13-Hedonist
14-Garble 15-Impute 18-Hallow

Multiple Choice
1-c. hedonist 2-c. florid 3-d. imperative 4-c. galvanized
5-b. imputed 6-b. heretic 7-d. gullible 8-a. flouted 9-d. fitful
10-a. garbled 11-a. furtive 12-a. frenetic 13-b. fulsome
14-c. gregarious 15-d. hallowed 16-c. iconoclast 17-a. hierarchy
18-c. impeached 19-d. impetuous 20-c. forlorn

Matching
1-O 2-F 3-S 4-T 5-H 6-K 7-I 8-P 9-G 10-L 11-R 12-B
13-N 14-E 15-M 16-Q 17-A 18-J 19-C 20-D

Chapter 6

Crossword Puzzle
Across: 1-Lampoon 3-Melancholy 6-Indigent 9-Laudable
11-Invective 16-Innocuous 17-Intransigence 18-Listless
Down: 1-Lethargy 2-Latent 4-Inundate 5-Inimical 7-Jargon
8-Incursion 10-Lackluster 12-Incongruous 13-Indomitable
14-Laconic 15-Malevolent 17-Insurgent

Multiple Choice
1-a. latent 2-c. jargon 3-d. lampoon 4-c. laconic 5-b. indigent
6-b. laudable 7-a. indomitable 8-b. inimical 9-a. malevolent
10-c. innocuous 11-d. incongruous 12-d. insurgent
13-a. intransigence 14-c. invective 15-a. lackluster
16-c. lethargy 17-d. listless 18-c. incursions 19-b. melancholy
20-b. inundated

Matching
1-A 2-I 3-B 4-M 5-R 6-F 7-S 8-G 9-P 10-K 11-C 12-T
13-D 14-E 15-N 16-J 17-L 18-O 19-H 20-Q

Chapter 7

Crossword Puzzle
Across: 2-Ostentatious 4-Noisome 6-Pique 8-Nomenclature
10-Nascent 11-Munificence 12-Piety 13-Omnipotent
15-Obfuscate 17-Nefarious 18-Paucity
Down: 1-Pernicious 3-Obsequious 5-Mnemonic 6-Palliate
7-Peregrinate 9-Ossify 12-Perfunctory 14-Parsimony
16-Panegyric

Multiple Choice
1-d. nefarious 2-c. nascent 3-b. piqued 4-d. pernicious
5-a. nomenclature 6-d. piety 7-b. obfuscating 8-c. peregrinate
9-c. obsequious 10-b. ostentatious 11-d. omnipotent 12-a. ossify
13-c. palliate 14-d. panegyric 15-a. parsimony 16-d. noisome
17-b. paucity 18-a. mnemonic 19-c. perfunctory
20-b. munificence

Matching
1-G 2-B 3-L 4-A 5-D 6-T 7-K 8-C 9-E 10-Q 11-J 12-P
13-I 14-F 15-R 16-H 17-O 18-M 19-N 20-S

Section 8

Crossword Puzzle
Across: 4-Pompous 7-Plausible 8-Relegate 9-Propensity
10-Purport 13-Prudent 14-Predilection 15-Prosaic 16-Pliant
17-Polemic
Down: 1-Procrastinate 2-Refurbish 3-Querulous 5-Precipitous
6-Redundant 7-Prodigious 11-Raucous 12-Quixotic 14-Prolific
15-Provocation

Multiple Choice
1-c. propensity 2-b. relegated 3-a. polemic 4-a. quixotic
5-b. prudent 6-c. precipitous 7-d. pliant 8-d. predilection
9-b. prolific 10-a. procrastinating 11-c. plausible
12-c. redundant 13-d. prodigious 14-d. prosaic 15-b. purported
16-a. refurbished 17-d. querulous 18-d. raucous 19-c. pompous
20-d. provocation

Matching
1-C 2-M 3-F 4-Q 5-N 6-I 7-A 8-J 9-O 10-R 11-G 12-L
13-B 14-S 15-H 16-E 17-T 18-D 19-P 20-K

Section 9

Crossword Puzzle
Across: 1-Spurious 4-Superfluous 5-Salient 6-Sophomoric 9-Ruthless 10-Remorse 11-Sententious 14-Sanctimonious 16-Stringent
Down: 2-Squalid 3-Supercilious 4-Soporific 5-Scapegoat 7-Respite 8-Seminal 9-Repugnant 10-Reticent 12-Reprobate 13-Succinct 15-Serene

Multiple Choice
1-d. soporific 2-d. succinct 3-b. sanctimonious 4-d. reprobate 5-a. reticent 6-c. superfluous 7-b. remorse 8-c. salient 9-c. scapegoat 10-a. sententious 11-a. supercilious 12-d. seminal 13-d. repugnant 14-b. serene 15-a. spurious 16-d. ruthless 17-b. squalid 18-c. sophomoric 19-c. stringent 20-c. respite

Matching
1-D 2-F 3-H 4-G 5-O 6-J 7-K 8-Q 9-L 10-I 11-A 12-R 13-M 14-P 15-N 16-T 17-C 18-E 19-S 20-B

Section 10

Crossword Puzzle
Across: 3-Viable 6-Tawdry 8-Temerity 9-Venerate 11-Waive 15-Wanton 16-Ungainly 17-Tenacity 18-Volatile 19-Threadbare
Down: 1-Validate 2-Undermine 4-Zany 5-Terse 7-Whet 10-Tentative 12-Vacillate 13-Voluminous 14-Unscathed 17-Tactless

Multiple Choice
1-d. whet 2-c. tawdry 3-d. threadbare 4-a. ungainly 5-b. tactless 6-c. waive 7-a. temerity 8-c. vacillates 9-b. undermined 10-d. tentative 11-c. unscathed 12-a. viable 13-a. validated 14-d. venerated 15-b. zany 16-d. wanton 17-d. volatile 18-c. tenacity 19-b. voluminous 20-b. terse

Matching
1-Q 2-M 3-F 4-B 5-L 6-I 7-H 8-J 9-O 10-R 11-N 12-P 13-K 14-T 15-A 16-D 17-G 18-S 19-E 20-C

Index

http://SolidA.net

Free Audio
O N L I N E
http://solida.net/

VOCABBUSTERS

study with style

Make

vocabulary
fun,
meaningful &
memorable

SOLIDA

Dusti D. Howell, Ph.D.
Deanne Howell, M.S.
Copyright © 2005 Solid A, Inc.

1654196

Made in the USA